In the Company
of Writers

My library was dukedom
large enough.
Shakespeare, *The Tempest*

In the Company of Writers

of Writers

A Life in Publishing

CHARLES SCRIBNER, JR.

Based on the Oral History by
JOEL R. GARDNER

CHARLES SCRIBNER'S SONS
NEW YORK
COLLIER MACMILLAN CANADA
TORONTO
MAXWELL MACMILLAN INTERNATIONAL
NEW YORK OXFORD SINGAPORE SYDNEY

CHARLES SCRIBNER'S SONS
Macmillan Publishing Company
866 Third Avenue, New York, NY 10022
Collier Macmillan Canada, Inc.

Library of Congress Cataloging-in-Publication Data
Scribner, Charles, 1921–
In the company of writers: a life in publishing/Charles Scribner, Jr.
p.   cm.
ISBN 0-684-19250-0
1. Scribner, Charles, 1921–   . 2. Publishers and publishing—
United States—Biography.   3. Authors and publishers—United States—
History—20th century.   4. Charles Scribner's Sons—History.   I. Title.
Z473.S39   1990
070.5'092—dc20
[B]   90-33309   CIP

Macmillan books are available at special discounts for bulk purchases
for sales promotions, premiums, fund-raising, or educational use.
For details, contact:

Special Sales Director
Macmillan Publishing Company
866 Third Avenue
New York, NY 10022

10 9 8 7 6 5 4 3 2 1

Printed in the United States of America

To my wife, JOAN—
*who has made every happy moment happier,
and every hardship easier to bear.*

Contents

Acknowledgments

I wish to express my deep gratitude to Joel R. Gardner, oral historian par excellence. Through his painstaking research in the Scribner Archives at the Princeton University Library, his probing and thoroughly engaging interviews for the Columbia Oral History Research Office, and his continued prompting, preparation, and organization of the transcripts, he elicited the memoir I would never have expected to write. To Jacques Barzun, whose unique literary skills and long-standing collaboration and friendship I have attempted to describe elsewhere herein, I owe no less a debt for his editorial expertise and assistance in translating the spoken word into publishable prose. My editor at Scribners, Robert Stewart, a "publisher's publisher" without peer, guided the project through all its stages with a gentle but sure hand. My son Charlie, the family archivist and art historian, commissioned the oral history and encouraged me to develop it into a book. Special thanks are also due to Terrence J. Mulry, who first suggested the Columbia Oral History, to production editor Tony Davis, copy editor Ann Bartunek, design director Janet Tingey, book designer Erich Hobbing, and art director Wendy Bass. Carol Wilson did an expert job of deciphering and typing, and Roberta Corcoran at Scribners made my conversion from publisher to author completely painless, indeed a source of pleasure.

List of Illustrations

❧

With Joan, our son Charlie, and our new daughter-in-law, Ritchie Markoe Scribner, at their Far Hills wedding, August 1979.

Our three sons, from left to right: Blair, Charlie, and John.

With Mary Hemingway at Scribners, April 1970, announcing the posthumous publication of *Islands in the Stream*.

With Joan and P. D. James in London.

On the ice, Joan entertained authors and other company alike—solo!

Growing Up
with Scribners

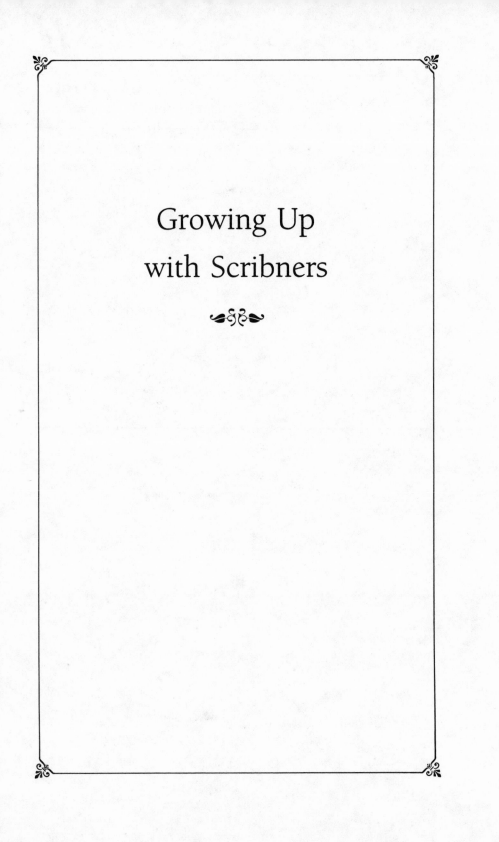

As far back as I have any definite childhood memories, I was aware that books were the business of our family. All my paternal relatives were involved in the publishing company, and it was soon made clear to me that as a great-grandson, a grandson, and a son, I had a destiny in publishing that could no more be changed than my gender.

I was born on July 13, 1921. I had a short-lived middle name, Hildreth, which was my mother's father's name. The weight of the Scribner family erased that from the records, although it is actually preserved on my birth certificate down in Quogue, Long Island, where I was born. Years later, my sister gave the name Hildreth to her first child, a daughter, so Hildreth has shifted from the male to the distaff side. It remains a family name. But I never used even the middle initial. It just withered away.

The season was summer, and in those days babies made their appearance in their mother's bed rather than in a hospital. It was a great dynastic act to have produced a son, and when my grandmother Scribner heard that I had been born, she said, "Make sure it's a boy. Doctors are very careless about these things."

I was really too young to know my grandfather well. He died in 1930, nine years after I was born, so my memories of him are those that a child would form. He had a lovely home at 9 East Sixty-sixth Street in New York City. His brother-in-law, Ernest Flagg, was a distinguished architect who renovated for my grandparents a house that had been on the site. It was charming, and my grandfather had a little study with some of his books there.

He was a businessman, interested in banking, and I think he served on the boards of several banks in New York. I don't honestly know how much of an intellectual he was; you can be a publisher without necessarily being an intellectual. He had many friends. He was a Princeton graduate, and all his classmates at Princeton, Class of 1875, loved one another sufficiently to reune regularly.

I recall him as quite a small man, with a mustache, blondish. They said that he had a withering glance, which made his employees shake with fear, but that wasn't apparent if you didn't work for the company. He was quite a bright, honorable, affectionate person.

He was very sweet to me. He was lame with sciatica, and once when I was sick in one of the places that my family rented in New York, he came up several flights of stairs to see me. But I was so young that there wasn't much he could do except say, "Hello, Charlie." It seems as if there were nothing more he could talk about at that stage of my life.

He was not very demonstrative. He carried himself with the slight stiffness of the Victorian and Edwardian regimes, when people were not always full of jokes. They took life seriously.

My grandmother Scribner was born into a distinguished artistic family, the Flaggs. Her brother Ernest, the architect, designed New York's first great skyscraper, the Singer Building; several buildings in Annapolis; and the Corcoran Art Gallery in Washington. He had been of fairly modest means as a young man, wellborn but not affluent. His first cousin Alice was married to Cornelius Vanderbilt II, grandson of the commodore. By some chance, Uncle Ernest was at the Vanderbilts' Fifth Avenue château when they were discussing plans to rearrange some rooms, and it was immediately apparent from Flagg's impromptu suggestions that he had a real gift for architecture: Vanderbilt staked him to an education at the Ecole des Beaux-Arts in Paris, a classical training that was of decisive importance in his career.

When Flagg came back to New York he had a handful of important commissions. He wasn't as innovative as Frank Lloyd Wright or Louis Sullivan; rather, he imported into the United States the French style and habits of the Beaux-Arts. All his buildings had a neoclassical touch; he brought into vogue their gabled roofs. You can see his style in the Scribner Building at 597 Fifth Avenue and in its predecessor at 155 Fifth Avenue. They have been declared city landmarks.

His father, and my grandmother's father, was Jared Flagg, a clergyman and prolific portraitist who lived in Hartford, Connecticut, and was a neighbor of Mark Twain. As a Flagg descendant, I inherited a marvelous little sketch of a young boy with a straw hat by Jared's eldest son, the portraitist Charles Noel Flagg, and I looked at it for years before it dawned on me that it was a painting of Twain's Tom Sawyer.

My grandmother, Louise Flagg, was a formidable person—strong-minded, snappy, stylish, extremely religious. A complete Anglophile, she loved English accents and ended up putting an extra r in America. She gave me fifty cents, my first real earnings, for memorizing the Collect each Sunday: at that rate I was prepared to learn all the Anglican Collects—with the Psalms thrown in for good measure. She and my grandfather had a home out in New Jersey, at Convent, in

Morris County, which they called "The Gables." She was an immensely devout Episcopalian with, at the same time, a great penchant for things Roman, and she built a little stone chapel in her garden, designed by Ernest Flagg. It was quite lovely, with a beautiful statue of the Virgin Mary—which wasn't exactly Protestant, but anyway, there she was. When my grandmother died, the family tore down the chapel. It was an architectural gem, but not wanting it to be desecrated by cocktail parties and the like, they got rid of it, to be preserved only in memories and photographs.

At "The Gables," my grandparents entertained a great deal and had many authors, such as John Galsworthy and Struthers Burt, come to visit. The famous sporting artist A. B. Frost was a neighbor and frequent guest—as well as illustrator for *Scribner's Magazine*. Other Scribners authors would come out for long weekends. In those informal days many books were published without benefit of contract. The publisher and the author were often close friends. To be fair, I'm not sure it was always good for the author to have the publisher as a close friend, and I wouldn't want to wax sentimental about that custom, but that's the way it was.

When we were living in New Jersey, we went regularly to my grandparents' house for Sunday lunch. They had a series of English prints of Shakespeare characters on the walls. I vividly remember one print of the fellow in *Henry V* who swallows a leek. It was quite impressive to a child arriving for lunch.

I am surprised that I don't recall my grandfather's library as "bookish." It was certainly not the library of a passionate reader. There were volumes and sets of books that he had published, which were not necessarily on the shelves to be read. He was a very good businessman who loved being a publisher, but I don't think books were an essential part of his private life. I remember beautiful bindings, but bindings are not books.

I was too young for my grandfather to take any interest in my reading, but I'm not sure that he would have been interested in anyone's reading. When my own sons were young, I wanted them to read the books that I had loved as a boy—the novels of Conrad and Dickens. With my eldest son, Charlie, I broke every rule: I gave him ten books that I had loved, and when he was about to go off to boarding school, I said I'd give him ten dollars a book or some such outrageously large sum if he would read them all. He now claims that that is what got him reading good books, such as *Lord Jim* and the novels of Thomas Hardy. Eventually he became a genuine scholar.

I often dream of my grandparents' house in New York city—poignant, vivid dreams. Oftentimes it involves my finding a room that goes off a staircase with a hidden door. There is a delightful room filled with books on the shelves and furniture that I didn't know was there. In another dream, I am again in my grandparents' house in the city and the little study opens on to the countryside, so that the city dissolves into a rural landscape with a farmyard and all kinds of bucolic sights.

I have thought much about what role such dreams may have. I call them romantic dreams, because they suggest that there are doors in familiar places that you haven't known were there, showing that reality has a way of opening up doors beyond the walls that confine us in life. These dreams express the romantic impulse for the unknown and also for literature, the yearning that fuels the creative imagination and scholarly curiosity alike.

My father was a very gentle man as well as a very traditional gentleman. He had a good sense of humor. He was also diffident. When my father died, I was in the navy. I went to the Scribners offices and looked at his desk. I discovered that in the dozen years between his father's death and his own, my father had never touched this desk that had been my grandfather's. Everything on it when his father sat there at the end of his life was still there when I saw it again, including a collection of Edith Wharton's short stories. My father had made a little nest in a drawer where he put cigarette filters and matches, but everything else was untouched. I came in with a much bolder spirit and pushed things around, but he had been so pious a son that he would not change the arrangement of his father's things. This curious Dickensian or Trollope-like touch exactly conveys his personality.

As a boy, my father had shown a flair for drawing, which raised the thought that he might grow up to be an artist like his Flagg forebears. To ward off that catastrophe, it was made certain that pencils, paints, and other art materials were kept out of his way. My father had a slight stammer all his life, and conceivably it was the result of parental efforts to pick and choose among his gifts. The Edwardians were capable of such measures. Many of that generation stammered, perhaps because they were corrected so much.

He had a fine, clear mind and could write a splendid letter, but he never thought of himself as intellectual. He was a nonintellectual with a fine intellect.

He never talked to me much until his last years; indeed, we had very little contact at all, though we'd go down to football games at Princeton, for he was a passionate Princetonian. But when I think of how close I've been to my own children, entering into their reading and their fun and their games as part of an active family life, I conclude that my father was not comfortable with children. Yet he certainly wasn't a disciplinarian. That was all left to my mother.

My mother was Vera Gordon Bloodgood. Hildreth Bloodgood, my grandfather, was a New Yorker of Dutch descent, and his wife, Julia Casey, was a Civil War general's daughter from Washington, D.C. My mother and father found each other through fox hunting, my mother being a tremendous rider who also competed in shows. Though not quite so brave and bold and skilled a rider, my father shared her passion for horses. Indeed, my father probably knew more about horses than my mother, but she rode them better.

My mother had a very strong personality, traditional as to manners and etiquette but with a keen sense of humor. She was not highly educated, having dropped out of the Chapin School in New York at sixteen. She had been given an opportunity to go to Russia, to the Court of Czar Nicholas II, where one of her cousins was the ambassador from Belgium. She spent a season in St. Petersburg, where she attended a party at the Winter Palace. She was not actually presented to the czar, but she watched as he, the czarina, and the czarevitch and grand-duchesses walked by. On winter evenings she went sledding and skating with the dashing Prince Yusupov, who later murdered Rasputin.

Though of limited education, my mother was intelligent and gifted. She sculpted without ever having lessons and produced some impressive bronzes of horses. My grandmother used to say that my mother "had never unpacked the first drawer of her trunk," and that may be true. She had no opportunity to develop her gifts at a time when few women were educated for full self-development like men.

My father commuted every night from New York to Far Hills, New Jersey. Our home, "Dew Hollow," was a neo-Georgian brick house with stables and horse pastures, an English garden and tennis court, set in two hundred acres of hunt country. In the winter, my parents rented a town house in New York, where we children would join them.

On many occasions my father and mother would go to England on publishing missions, and my sister and I would be left with our grandmother and grandfather Scribner. I enjoyed this because it gave me a chance to see my grandfather and learn to appreciate him, despite his shyness toward children. It's a nice memory.

My mother's father and mother had died before I could know them. But they had had a country house in New Marlboro, Massachusetts, and we spent many summer vacations there.

My sister, Julia, three years older than I, was a very intelligent young woman who also never went to college. It was a shame, for I think she would have jumped at the chance. Nonetheless, she became a well-read woman who loved books, music, and art. We had not much in common until I got out of boarding school and had begun to write a little. Then she grew very supportive. We had fun with music—though I had no voice at all—and when Julia was taking voice lessons, I used to sing Siegmund in *The Valkyrie* to accompany her in practice. That was the extent of my singing career. I can still hear "*Winterstürme wichen dem Wonnemond.*"

My family's chief sport was horseback riding. One afternoon in New Marlboro, we were all riding through an alder swamp when my sister's horse went down into a bog, rolled over her, and broke her hip right at the top, the worst possible break. My family sent for an expert orthopedic surgeon from New York to set the leg. Well, this *Herr Professor* made the long trip and set the leg, but he didn't put it in traction—an incredible oversight. Even Caesar's legions set bones in traction! The local country doctor asked, "Aren't you going to put it in traction?" The authoritative reply was, "No, the cast will hold it in place."

Almost immediately, the leg muscles turned the bone around and shortened my sister's height by about half an inch, so she had to go into the hospital afterwards and have her leg rebroken surgically. It shattered her health. Up to that time she had been something of a tomboy; afterwards she was almost continually ill.

My sister realized early in life that men were the chosen people in our Trollope-like family. They ran the business, and the women had little or nothing to say or do about it. So she kept wishing she were a boy. In fact, she became a Boy Scout under the name of Julius Scribner; she bought canteens and hunting knives and rifles. It was quite sad.

In due course, she married a clergyman and professor at General Theological Seminary in New York. In her early forties she was stricken with cancer and died, leaving four young children aged four to fifteen. Hers was a tragic life in many respects. Besides her gifts as an amateur musician, she was a good photographer and she also wrote well. Shortly before she became ill she edited and introduced an anthology of the works of Marjorie Kinnan Rawlings, who had befriended her many years before and had appointed Julia her literary executor.

As a child, I had as nanny an old Irish spinster named Cece. She was totally uneducated, but I loved her more dearly than I did my family—not a rare phenomenon in those days. As a result I think I was a bit of a sissy, for a nanny's job depends on the overprotection of her charges, and since my parents were shaken by the kidnapping of the Lindbergh baby only a few miles away, they gave Cece ironclad instructions on child rearing. She was almost illiterate but could read the daily prayers in her Catholic missal.

Thanks to her constant care I was for a brief time brought up as a Catholic. My family took it all in a laissez-faire spirit. I had a crucifix over my bed, but my father paid no attention. My mother noticed but she understood the bond between a child and a nurse, and she didn't resent the obvious fact of my great affection for Cece. Since they did not worry about it, my early Catholicism seems to have had no lasting effect.

Though my parents were not profoundly religious, religion had a place in their lives. They were conventional Episcopal churchgoers of their era, and my father was a vestryman in the Church of St. Luke's in Gladstone, New Jersey. I later went to St. Paul's School in Concord, New Hampshire, an Episcopal institution. Eventually I became the senior warden of St. Bartholomew's Church in New York. Yet I do not think of myself as a naturally religious person. Rather, I have had a series of responsibilities placed on me that I have fulfilled, some out of a sense of duty, others with a sense of dedication and joy. The former I have done because I felt that they were expected of me as a member of a family in which tradition and continuity were of great importance.

Such, too, was my relation to publishing. It had been settled, so I grew up without some of the freedoms that others enjoy who can paddle their own canoe. Yet I soon found things that interested me enormously and that I was able to pursue, such as the history of science, which I taught myself; so the story has a happy ending after all.

Far Hills, New Jersey, was a fashionable community peopled by devotees of fox hunting. I rode because everybody rode, but I hated it like the dickens. We had to go out on paralyzingly hot days on dusty roads, with flies all over us. Often as I rode along I would mentally measure the distance and time it would take to get back home. My mother would come up from behind and strike me on the back with a riding crop—not harshly, but decisively, not because she read my mind, but because she had seen light between my knees and the withers of the horse. Eventually I stopped because I got terribly allergic to horses and couldn't even go near the stables. That gave me a reprieve from all horsey things. The body isn't always fooled.

Life in Far Hills was extraordinary. Everyone had about the same degree of wealth and the same interests, and everybody's home was by common consent everybody else's. If my father felt in the afternoon that he would like a cocktail, he would simply go into the nearest house of a friend, and the butler would appear with a drink on a silver tray. That was very hard on me, for a curious reason. I grew up without a developed sense of property, which one needs in order to be a tactful human being. No one had much sense of ownership. My mother was generous in a *beau geste* way, but at the same time she might arbitrarily take something of mine. Property was something loosely held. Consequently, when I got to boarding school, I had a grim awakening about the social facts of life, namely that other people have their own possessions. I think I learned that lesson well, but it was an awkward apprenticeship.

I went off to St. Paul's in 1934 when I was thirteen years old. I had never been one night away from home before, so I had a hard time. Moreover, I was a little guy, and adjustment was quite traumatic. The school was run on the rigorous English model and I was quite homesick for a long time; I had led too sheltered a life.

Before St. Paul's, I had attended a little country school in Far Hills, the Somerset Hills School. It afforded only a poor education, the kind one gets when the teacher tries to do more than he can manage. We often read books beyond our comprehension, we memorized rules of arithmetic beyond our understanding, and we learned by rote the Latin prepositions—*ad, ante, con, de,* and so on—and their appropriate cases. The school was run by a Dickensian clergyman and his wife who looked as if they had stepped out of a Cruikshank drawing. I subsequently heard that the master had a fondness for drink; it may have contributed to the pervasive unpredictability of the program. I was a faithful student and got good grades by dint of will, but I was learning without understanding. It was not until later that I got a firm grasp on *what* I was learning.

The five years I spent at St. Paul's were hardly a jamboree; I got a very good education. Those New England prep schools were athletic aristocracies, however, and since I was no athlete, I opted—like Louis Auchincloss at Groton—to be an intellectual, to pursue a life of reading and study and ruminating. It is still the major part of my life.

St. Paul's gave good training in the classics, so that I arrived at Princeton an almost full-fledged intellectual—at least as fully fledged as I then desired. I loved learning. But for the family publishing business, I probably would have become a teacher. I was later asked to come back to Princeton as a Woodrow Wilson Fellow in the graduate school. But the family tie held fast. Looking back, I have no regrets, because I have found a happy intellectual life through book publishing.

In the course of my childhood I may have once or twice visited my grandfather or father at Scribners, in order to view a parade on Fifth Avenue. One other (official) visit during childhood was to the Scribner Press, a few blocks south, where I had a tour of the bindery and printing plant. The result was that I wanted my own printing press. My grandfather gave me a little job press, and somebody was sent out from the company to show me how to work it.

An aunt of mine gave me a Chinese story translated into English—a saccharine, sentimental tale called "A Secret Land." I set it in type on my printing press. I worked and worked and worked, and when I had "A Secret Land" all printed in quarto, I showed it to my sister. That reviewer pointed out that it read "S-e-r-e-t" instead of "S-e-c-r-e-t." The humiliation was more than I could stand; thus ended a budding career in the printing trade.

The Scribner plant had been no less intimidating. The elevators worked on a hydraulic system that shot them up from floor to floor with accelerations not even New Yorkers were accustomed to. In the basement were great steam engines that made electricity to run the presses. On the upper floors the books were manufactured. One floor housed the composing machines that set the type, both the complex Monotype machines that were programmed by a punched tape, something like a player piano, and the simpler Linotype machines that cast whole lines on individual metal slugs. I was given one of those slugs as a souvenir. Not far from the Linotypes was a caldron the size and shape of a bathtub, brimming and bubbling with molten type metal. A piece of paper brought near the surface would break into flame. I still can recollect the shudder I felt at the sight.

In addition to the machines and their users, there was a staff of rather elderly men who set type letter by letter in the way it was done beginning with Gutenberg. I was struck by the fact that they had to set each line as the mirror image of what would appear in print.

On the floor that contained the bindery, the air was saturated with the smell of binder's glue, an intoxicating aroma for book lovers who can get a whiff of it in new books. There the printed sheets were folded, gathered, stitched, and cased on a clattering assembly line that might have inspired Rube Goldberg. It was so big, and there were so many people—it was an awesome experience for a child.

It was a little frightening, too, to reflect that all this meant Scribners. I felt terribly diminished by the scope of the operation and the thought that I was expected to play some role in it. I was intensely aware that I was the next in line. My given name, Charles Scribner III, played up the dynastic aspect of the family and the business, which in turn clouded my sense of freedom about the foreseeable future. (Actually, I was the *fourth* Charles, but at my birth only the live ones were counted and numbered; this tradition of moving up the numerical ladder has caused endless confusion, as both my father and my son have also carried the Roman III.)

I well remember my first meeting with an author. One evening before the grown-ups had sat down to dinner, the famous cowboy artist and writer Will James, who was visiting my parents, came up to my room and, sitting on the side of the bed, drew a little sketch of a cow horse's foal on the back of a piece of my father's stationery and gave it to me. I was moved and captivated by the charm of the drawing. James's book *Smoky* won our first Newbery Medal for children's literature and it is still in print on Scribners' current list.

Another visitor was Willard Huntington Wright, who had earned a reputation as a learned art critic before he embarked on his career as a writer of detective stories under the pen name S. S. Van Dine. After his recovery from a heart attack, the doctors had forbidden him any serious reading, and during this convalescence he read dozens of these books. On the basis of his analysis of the genre, he became convinced that he could do better than most of the ones he had read. His editor, Maxwell Perkins, gave him a three-book contract for crime novels on the strength of outlines alone, and in so doing signed up one of the most successful authors of the thirties.

I remember the Wrights paying a visit to our house. My own great interest at the time was electricity. I had stretched a wire around the side of our house to rig a little telephone system between the wings. When the Wrights were shown into their room, Mr. Wright spotted the wire and in the spirit of his great detective, Philo Vance, he hinted at the possibility of some sinister plot. He proceeded to open the window and climb out on the roof to see where the wires led to. All this was inexplicable to my mother and father, who knew nothing about the telephone system. But I was absolutely delighted by the performance and felt I had met a real-life hero.

Earlier, at the age of seven, I had tried my hand at writing a detective story, entitled "The Old Brick House of Mystery." One of my grandfather's authors persuaded him to have it printed and bound—all eight pages of it. It was my first experience on the writer's side of the publishing table.

Although my parents visited Hemingway on several occasions, including two trips to the Finca Vigía, his residence in Cuba, I do not think he ever visited them at home. He was usually comfortable only on his own turf.

Marjorie Rawlings was a frequent visitor, and her book, *The Yearling*, was one of Scribners' great successes. Marjorie became an intimate friend of the family, and (as I recalled earlier) eventually appointed my sister as her executor. Marjorie was as pleasant and down to earth as her books would suggest, even though on one occasion I remember her saying at lunch that "art transmogrifies life." It was out of character for her to use such a jawbreaker; she may have felt that the occasion demanded something profound.

That she was a tough-minded woman was clear when she met Ernest Hemingway; they hit it off wonderfully. She later made a penetrating analysis of Hemingway's character, weighing his sensitivity against his braggadocio, and putting into words what is probably one of the best characterizations of Hemingway. She understood that Hemingway was divided between two worlds: the world of sporting things, in which he had to be tough and a great sportsman, and the world of literature, in which he was a truly sensitive artist. She was a very perceptive woman and a formidable writer.

On one occasion the novelist Thomas Wolfe paid a weekend visit to our home. I was away at boarding school and in fact never did meet him, then or later. On that particular occasion the Scribners had another guest, a peppery old friend and former master of foxhounds who was at least as opinionated and argumentative as Wolfe himself. After my mother and father had retired for the night, the two men sat in the library arguing and theorizing and certainly imbibing, into the wee hours. Having worked up an appetite, they managed to find their way into the kitchen, where they helped themselves to generous portions of chopped meat, finding it quite delicious. In the morning the cook came to my mother in a quandary. Somehow all the raw meat that had been set out to feed the dogs had vanished during the night—pounds of it. I must confess that I have never been able to separate the details of that midnight meal from my mental picture of the towering author of *Look Homeward, Angel*.

One of the special benefits of growing up in a publishing family was to be surrounded by many of the paintings and drawings that had been commissioned to illustrate various Scribner books. In those days the publisher usually acquired the original artwork along with the copyright. Some paintings were returned to artists, some were given to schools, and some found their way to our house. Several of the paintings produced by N. C. Wyeth for *The Boy's King Arthur* were acquired in that way. I vividly remember that on the wall behind the spiral staircase there hung the ghostly arm of the Lady of the Lake as she reached out of the water to give King Arthur his great sword Excalibur.

I have an original black-and-white watercolor from that era by A. B. Frost. It shows the Pickwick Club at Dingley Dell at Christmastime, with Mr. Pickwick sliding across the ice. Finding it absolutely charming, I had the inspiration, one Christmas, of having that watercolor copied and put on the shopping bags of the Scribner Book Store.

So past and present churn around and bring up different thoughts and images. One of my later reading-reference works was a large set of critical and biographical essays on American writers. Again, I found a tiny advertisement from my great-grandfather's time about a series on American writers that could almost have been an advertisement for what I was to do generations later. My great-grandfather had written to Thoreau to ask him to send some material for this series, and Thoreau had written in his diary that he'd heard from a man named Scribner and described what my great-grandfather wanted. These little discoveries of history delight me, providing as they do the threads that add color to the fabric of tradition.

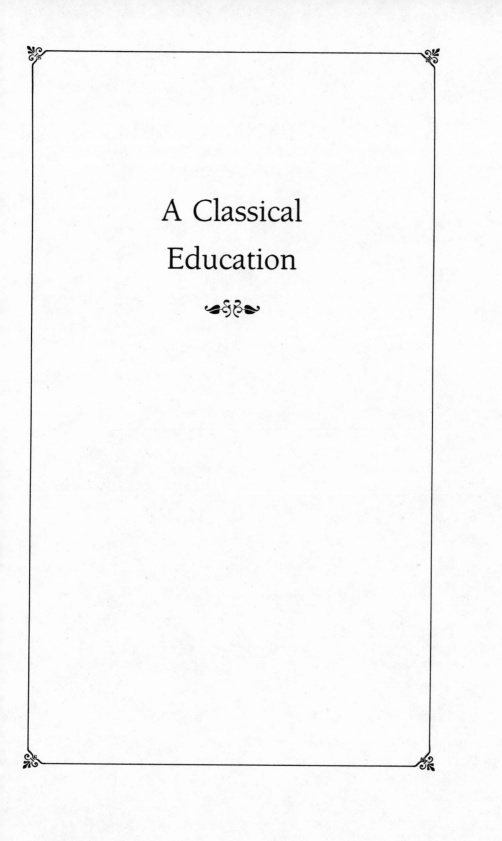

A Classical
Education

I started reading for the love of it when I was a student at St. Paul's. I then read, as every true book lover reads, with a kind of pleasure that is akin to eating. But it's a unique pleasure. You have the story and the style and the binding of the book in your hand; it's an enchantment. You crave reading something well written, savoring every page.

I owe a debt of gratitude to the schoolboy I was then. He was willing to bite the bullet when it came to the hard parts and the dull parts of learning Latin. The effort he made then bore fruit abundantly in the years that lay ahead. I have only gratitude for that former self and for his somewhat later self, who had the good sense to major in the classics at Princeton and to begin the study of Greek there. Fortunately he was able to learn enough to afford at least a glimpse of the unique glories of the ancient world and its literatures. I hope those earlier selves will not think I have squandered the intellectual capital accumulated by their efforts.

When I was a schoolboy there was comparatively little debate about the importance of Latin in the curriculum. This was in the good old days of College Board examinations, in which Latin through Caesar was a fixture. From Maine to

California, children who were college-bound took two to three years of Latin. How lucky they were! Outstanding institutions like Oak Park High School in Illinois, where Ernest Hemingway got his education, went all out to make the study of Latin a truly humanistic experience. The Oak Park school had a special Latin Room with Roman chairs and a stone desk. I don't know what Hemingway's views were on these objects and that curriculum, but Latin may have contributed to the simple and direct style that was the hallmark of his writing.

Of course, some strong-minded individuals rebelled. Winston Churchill was one. By his own testimony, he refused to take seriously a language in which one learned how to address a table. Yet one cannot read any of Churchill's speeches without seeing the extent of his indebtedness to the oratorical tradition of Cicero and Demosthenes, which also nurtured the neoclassical thought and culture of Western civilization. Cicero himself might have been glad to borrow a phrase or two from Churchill. His famous battle cry, ". . . blood, toil, tears and sweat," sounds like authentic Latin: "*Sanguis, labor, lacrimae, sudorque.*"

In the advanced "forms" at St. Paul's School, the teaching was generally taken over by senior masters. In some cases that was a nerve-racking experience without offsetting educational benefits. I have Proustian recollections of reading Cicero at the feet—and to some extent under the heel—of an otherwise cheerful little man named Peck. His classes were held in an antiquated room several floors up in the schoolhouse. There, three walls were faced with blackboards, and at each session Mr. Peck would deal out to each of us a three-by-five card from a thumb-worn deck. Each card bore a sentence in Latin or English to be translated into the reciprocal language. It was a sudden-death situation in which one mistake meant a grade of fifty percent and two mistakes zero.

A story lay behind the rigor of Mr. Peck's method. Apparently as a young teacher he had suffered the humiliation of having a form-wide examination failed by most of his class. Then and there he took a solemn Roman oath with himself that this would never happen again. We were on the operative side of that oath, and, while we did well in translating Cicero, the substance of his orations was soon forgotten.

There simply has to be an element of charm if learning is to stick. I can remember looking out the window, too high up to see the ground, and watching the tops of the great school pines as they stirred and swayed in the wind. That was in 1936, and in that year the Italian government—Mussolini's government—issued a set of stamps commemorating the Roman poet Horace. I remember them vividly and was struck that something so exquisitely beautiful could be related to a literature that seemed to me so lifeless at the time.

But now, just recently, about a year or so ago, I went down to a stamp dealer's and bought those stamps, out of curiosity, and they're on my desk at home now. On the stamp one sees a bit of Fascist propaganda behind the appropriation of the motto *Dulce et decorum est, pro patria mori*—but then Horace was himself extolling dying for one's native land. At any rate, here they are, little relics of my Latin years.

Mr. Peck was of the old school, teaching Latin the way they teach dogs tricks with hot irons. It was a grim experience; one was always over a precipice. To us, Peck's bad boys, he was the epitome of a martinet, though outside the classroom he was a jovial, kindly person, who cannot have thought of himself as being in any way cruel.

I was wearying of Latin and ready to drop it if I could, but my last year brought about a dramatic reversal of feeling. In the fall of 1938 I was invited to sign up for a special course in Roman literature in which we read selections from Livy, Plautus, Horace, and Catullus. The teacher, a man named Morris, loved these works. He loved Virgil and Horace and Catullus, the plays of Plautus and Terence with a contagious enthusiasm. Almost everything I learned that year has stuck in my mind. I can still imagine Horace throwing another log on the fire and opening another bottle of wine, or Catullus sailing his little skiff.

That set fire to my curiosity about the classics; this man Morris was a teacher who was also a humanist. One would not have expected to find him such because in other ways he was of the old school, rather severe and humorless. But he did pass on that little torch of his enthusiasm to me, so that when I went to Princeton I had a running start on classical studies. I was able to go into an advanced course because the authors I'd been reading come late in the curriculum. I was so fired up that I took up Greek.

When I arrived at Princeton in the fall of 1939, I was impressed by the maturity of the life and the education. It was like passing out of one room into a much wider one—into the real life of the mind. It was wonderful. I had a good grounding in English literature, too, and was able to take nothing but sophomore courses—with satisfaction and success. I decided to major in classics.

At that time, the university was enjoying something of a humanistic revival. The undergraduate curriculum provided programs and courses designed to give a broader view of the arts. Whitney Oates and Eugene O'Neill, Jr., wrote a textbook called *Greek Drama in Translation* and it formed the basis of Oates's course called "Classics in Translation," which I found a very good introduction. We read Homer in the Butcher-and-Lang version. In the later classics courses, in the original language, the method and syllabus did not differ greatly from those of St. Paul's, but the richness of the interpretation was incomparably greater.

Whitney Oates was a committed humanist. With Theodore Meyer Greene, Francis Godolphin, and Asher Hines, he was a founder of the Divisional Program in the Humanities. Those were all big names at Princeton, and they drew me into their orbit. Princeton has a single faculty, so under-classmen have the benefit of instruction by professors who also teach the graduate courses. Their scholarship enables them to bring the undergraduates the true meaning and relevance of the masterpieces they read. For example, in the course on Horace, I acquired an understanding of poetic technique that I have never forgotten or had to revise. It was an enormous feast of the intellect to be there.

My only disappointment was that I really had wanted to go into mathematics, deeply if possible, and no place could have given me better mathematics than Princeton. But I went to an introductory session, and the instructor spent the entire time explaining how the course was going to be graded, what weight would be attached to the different parts of the tests, and so forth. It was so off-putting that I dropped math once and for all and went into a creative writing course taught by Allen Tate.

Some might say that I'd had a happy escape, but I wish I had kept on with mathematics, because since that time my interest in it has grown even stronger. I do not pretend that I have an authentic mathematical talent, but I could have learned in college far more easily than I have been able to do independently, and I regret the missed opportunity.

Nothing came of my creative writing class, because I obviously wasn't meant to be a creative writer. I have written a lot, and have had a great deal of fun; I have tried to write with style, but it is clear that if I had had a more decided writing ability, I would have pursued it.

I did not greatly like my class with Allen Tate. It was the heyday of the New Criticism, which sought to downplay the older literature in favor of the new, exemplified by Ezra Pound, T. S. Eliot, and their school, and Tate was their advocate. He was always scoring off on Shelley and Byron and Browning and giving Edmund Wilson his share of hard knocks; if only the Agrarians (as the new school was also known) had reason and virtue on their side.

This doctrine gave me no pleasure or profit. I came to feel that one of the blessings of learning literature through the classics was that it protected me from the New Criticism and its aesthetics. Its adherents defined literature so narrowly that only a few writers were allowed in the gate. By contrast, reading Horace and Virgil and the Greek tragedians with Princeton's outstanding classicists gave me a broader conception of literature, and this in turn was a liberating experience. Consequently, I took only one literature course at Princeton, a class in Milton, with a Professor Savage. I had a considerable advantage in my classical preparation since Milton was neoclassical. I could see the pattern of Greek arguments in his works and was able to contribute to the discussions, with the instructor's approval and encouragement whenever I came up with some *aperçu*.

In the rest of what went on at Princeton, I was not involved. Far Hills was less than an hour away, and I went home to my family every weekend. Consequently, I missed all the real college life. My Princeton years were exclusively academic. I loved the place for its learning and its faith in the life of the mind. I am not without some sentimental memories, but acquiring knowledge is what meant most to me.

At that time the famous classical scholar Henry Prescott, on leave from the University of Chicago, was a visiting professor at Princeton. I was fortunate enough to have several courses with him. Disdaining conventional textbook versions of many of the Roman elegies, he would mimeograph and give out his own versions. He was scornful of all translations that failed to catch the Roman spirit as he felt it. Among his emendations of earlier texts, I remember especially his pointing out that Catullus's little ode to Lesbia's sparrow ought to be combined with the very short piece that follows it and speaks of the girdle of Venus. This suggestion was based on an extremely erotic interpretation of the paired pieces, the separation of the two having probably been made in the Middle Ages by some monastic copyist who had failed to get the point—or, on the contrary, had got it all too well.

Prescott had other revelations about the Roman elegies. I had naïvely imagined that the lady loves immortalized by the poets, while obviously emancipated, were on an equal social footing with their lovers—girls next door, so to speak. It came as a shock to learn that all those Lesbias, Cynthias, and Corinnas were professionals: they were not in it for the poetry. And the touching plight of the poet, cruelly scorned by the girl or thwarted by the implacable gatekeeper, was a convention taken over by the Romans from the Hellenistic Greeks.

Prescott brought into the class, while I was yet but a sophomore, the standards of learning and philology of a graduate school. It was thrilling to try to discover the exact meaning of the words and their intention. He was bent on eliciting the *mot juste* in translating, and I loved it.

When it came to Lucretius, I found him an antidote to any disillusionments. No one could question the sincerity of

Lucretius—that is what gives so much force to his art—and in later years when I became an amateur scholar in the history of science, I was interested to note how the *De Rerum Natura* kept the theory of atoms alive in Western thought. It survived for many years as a philosophical doctrine, it was provisionally accepted by Newton in the seventeenth century, brought into the rising science of chemistry by Dalton in the early nineteenth century, and finally established as a physical reality by the young Einstein in 1905.

During my Princeton years Reinhold Niebuhr was a Scribner author, just then writing his *Nature and Destiny of Man.* Being myself interested in the history of ideas, I had bought a copy of Lovejoy's *Documentary History of Primitivism and Related Ideas in Antiquity* and I gave it to Niebuhr as possibly useful in the writing of his book. He was grateful and said to me, "This book is going to be the most wonderful grist for my mill."

This little incident was my first exertion of influence on one of our authors before I actually joined Scribners. I think he kindly mentioned it in a little footnote.

People at Princeton like Asher Hines and Whitney Oates were much taken with Niebuhr's ideas, and I was able to bring down page proofs of his book to those of my professors who were anxious to read it as soon as possible. I must say that Niebuhr had a tremendous influence on me. I was asked once to name the five books that meant most to me in my life, and one of the five was Niebuhr's *Moral Man and Immoral Society.*

Because of the nature of my studies, I had an opportunity —in fact an obligation—to write a senior thesis of greater length than usual. It was on Stoicism and Epicureanism as factors in seventeenth- and eighteenth-century literature and philosophy and it was almost a small book. I researched it in the library, and although I was supposed to be guided from start to finish, I preferred to be a free lance, and put the thing together in my own way; my sponsoring professors allowed it.

Oates was my mentor and I was one of his special protégés. We remained friends afterwards, and I later published a little book of his on Aristotle. A strong-minded classicist, he wouldn't brook any sentimentality or wishy-washyness. He taught graduate-school rigor, and I can't thank him enough for inculcating it into my youthful mind.

The study of any language other than one's own offers the advantage of enabling one to step out of one's native ways of thought into those of another; it protects one from parochialism while it also strengthens one's grasp of the native language. Translating out of Greek and Latin did more to teach me English than anything I had ever done or could do. Besides, there was a beauty in Greek that was intoxicating. I can't explain it. It is linked with the alphabet the words are written in, and their sound, and something that I could almost taste, a physical thing.

Robert Goheen was an undergraduate at Princeton a couple of years ahead of me. He was a *Wunderkind*, and all my teachers were always telling me what Bob Goheen had done. I grew very much aware of him, since we were both in the humanities department, both classicists and protégés of Whitney Oates. This led to our becoming good friends. Latin and Greek and this friendship led again, much later, to a golden experience, the kind that happens only once in a lifetime. I had been reading some Horace just for the fun of it, and went to Princeton for a meeting. Bob Goheen was then president of the university, and he mentioned that he wanted to know something about a poem of Horace. By a sublime coincidence, I had been reading that poem the day before. My reply to his question at large stunned everybody, myself included. I never told him of this coincidence and he must have thought I was a great classicist in the German tradition.

I also took a good deal of German at Princeton, and I had studied French from the time I was a little boy. Being a very poor linguist, I never could speak French fluently. I was taught in the bad old way, by learning only to read silently—no conversation. My German was of the same sort. Still, I'm grateful for both. I've done a little translating just for the pleasure of it. Not long ago I translated a book of satirical German essays, and a book of French mathematical and logical puzzles, as exercises to help keep my reading knowledge green.

Humanistic studies should not be thought of as a curriculum at all but as a point of view toward all departments of knowledge. For instance, you can have a humanistic treatment of the history of physics. If you want to learn from the Scribner reference book, the *Dictionary of Scientific Biography*, you are learning something from a humanistic point of view. If you want to know what Einstein did, how he went about it, why he did it, and what the background of his thought was, what that dictionary provides is historical, biographical, and hence humanistic information. If you want to know formulas and how to handle relativity technically and use it in theoretical or experimental physics, then you go to another kind of reference book.

One of the most important things I have learned, from either a book or a teacher, was written by a man named Josiah Willard Gibbs (1839–1903), who was perhaps the greatest American physicist. He was an unrecognized genius in science for a long time and better known in Europe than in his own country. Somebody wrote him a letter praising one of his papers. He answered that he was grateful for the praise, because his work was in a theoretical field and it is hard to see the merits of theoretical work. They are not apparent on the surface, but the object of theoretical research in every department of knowledge is to find the point of view from which the subject appears in its greatest simplicity.

That remark has been to me a kind of Rosetta Stone. I have even translated it into Latin because I think it's the one key to any department of knowledge. God gave us a brain to make things simple, not complicated.

Phi Beta Kappa meant a lot to me when I got it—in my junior year. This and other honors were a sign that I had had a good career at Princeton, happier than at St. Paul's. What I most appreciate is that without Princeton my subsequent career would not have been possible. Looking back on those undergraduate years I see them as a golden period, a period in which I fell in love with learning. These words have a pompous air, no doubt, but being true and important, they had better be set down.

After Pearl Harbor, when many undergraduates were accelerating their studies so as to enter the armed services, the classics continued to play a role in my life. Francis Godolphin of the Princeton Classics Department recruited me as a candidate for a cryptanalytic group in the U.S. Navy known as OP20-G. I went into the navy in 1943, immediately after graduation.

The team I was assigned to was responsible for the decipherment of the principal Japanese naval code, JN25, which was the basis for many of our victories in the Pacific and contributed to the virtual annihilation of the Japanese merchant marine. Japan was doomed before the end of the war because it couldn't import any food: we were sinking all its ships. A Japanese captain sailing back to the homeland would give what was called a *shogo ichi*, his known position for the next ten days, and he would never get home.

For the young college men and women on our team, the work was a species of graduate-school experience. We worked under several professors from various universities, including some of my former teachers at Princeton. Clearly, the belief was that as translators, classicists would have a bent for cryptanalysis. One colleague in OP20-G was a young Harvard classicist named John Moore. During a particularly difficult problem of decipherment, I remember, he wrote an aphorism from ancient Greek, "Under every stone there is a scorpion." Everybody felt its aptness.

All told, I spent five years in cryptanalytic work, during both World War II and the Korean War. In spite of unavoidable frustrations, I enjoyed it. When earlier I had struggled to assemble the scattered words of a Horatian ode into a correct and coherent whole, I never thought that the task (which I still do not find easy) would help me some day to pinpoint the position of an ill-fated Japanese freighter in the middle of the Pacific Ocean.

Stationed in Washington, D.C., in the Navy Communications Annex, I felt strangely alone; I had very few friends in the city and the team worked on a swing shift. I kept largely to myself, only occasionally going home to New Jersey on weekend leave. Of Washington and its many attractions I saw virtually nothing. I visited none of its art galleries. It was as though I had flown over the capital but never landed.

I never learned Japanese, but I learned many of its word patterns and their meanings. That sufficed: we weren't decoding Shakespeare's sonnets. Not many Japanese translators were available when the war started; our unit had two, who were Seventh-Day Adventists—peaceful, lovely, elderly men—and they helped us with Japanese meanings. These gentle men wouldn't kill a fly, but here they were, contributing essential information that would lead to the sinking of a freighter or capital ship.

I felt also the irony of being stationed in wartime Washington when the action was in the Pacific. I thought that any day I would be transferred to active service. I hardly unpacked my suitcase. But I was kept there for the duration.

At the end of the war I received an invitation from Whitney Oates, who was setting up the Woodrow Wilson Fellowships to attract young people to the life of teaching and scholarship in the universities. I was in the first group of recruits, along with Bob Goheen. It was a difficult decision to make, but I chose to join Scribners instead. I thought it would break my parents' hearts if I didn't go into the firm. In retrospect, my judgment is that I did not give up as much as it then seemed, for I was entering a business that was to provide many of the intellectual satisfactions and pleasures one associates with academic life. Indeed, as a publisher I probably made more of a conscious effort to keep fresh my intellectual interests.

I returned to Washington to serve again during the Korean War. By then I had had some publishing experience. Hiram Haydn, editor of *The American Scholar*, had started a biographical series for Scribners called The Twentieth-Century Library, and one of its books was on Einstein. I had the job of editing that book, in the course of which I realized that I had no true understanding of relativity theory. I was unhappy about that lacuna, so during my second stay in Washington, by which time I was married, I began to study physics, and I finally managed to grasp Einstein's relativity.

As I couldn't take any work home, because it was all classified, I had the evenings free for reading and study. I had read a book written for the layman by James Bryant Conant called *Science and Common Sense*, which made a deep impression on me. I got some of the books he recommended and immersed myself in physics and the history of ideas. I also began to read *The Journal of the History of Ideas*, edited by

Philip P. Wiener. And there was *Isis*, the journal of the history of science. Both were important to me then and were in time to result in my publishing major reference works in the history of science and of ideas: the *Dictionary of Scientific Biography* in sixteen volumes and the *Dictionary of the History of Ideas* in five—but that is another chapter. In the reading done in Washington I had neither a practical nor a commercial idea of its future significance. Yet it turned out to be the basis of the most important contribution I have made to Scribners as editor and publisher.

A Young
Publisher

M y father never gave me, by fire or water, a baptism into publishing; he wasn't a baptizing type. I don't think he would have known what to say or do. He adopted the sink-or-swim method, so the first month I was at Scribners, my assignment was to deal with Ernest Hemingway on an illustrated edition of *A Farewell to Arms*. It was a good place to start, but in hindsight it seems incredible that I should have been entrusted with that job. I had to do everything besides: I wrote copy for advertisements, I read scripts, I wrote jacket flaps—the lot. I never had one blessed minute of instruction from anybody, in any branch of the business. I was expected to pick it up.

When I got into the business side, I began to learn brand new things on my own, but had to learn by recapitulation, which was wasteful. I knew nothing about business balance sheets; it was like deciphering all over again, and it was a poor way to learn. The whole experience brings into question the way that one generation teaches another. I was no more prepared at age thirty to take over Scribners than to land on the moon. I did not even know how much I didn't know.

Old retainers would show me how to do this or that, but I had far too much responsibility. When I think of the ads I wrote and the awful reports on books submitted, stiff and pedantic, it makes me squirm.

In my first days at Scribners, Max Perkins was still there. I knew him only briefly; it was the last year of his life. My father adored him as a colleague, really loved him; they ate lunch together nearly every day at Cherio's. Perkins was already a legend—amusing, talented, and utterly charming. But by the time I arrived he was going downhill very fast. He drank too much, perhaps in response to his earlier association with Thomas Wolfe's Homeric imbibing. Things reached a point where Max was accepting for publication manuscripts that earlier he would have declined. He was outraged, I think, by my lack of know-how about publishing. He once said to me, "You've got to learn to like the books we do." And I said to myself, "Well, some day I'll do the books I like."

Perkins was a great editor, yet he retained a sense of the amateur about himself; it was an essential part of his greatness and endeared him to his authors. He wasn't a know-it-all in any way, but his talents and his myth made it hard for Scribners to build on his success; the young editors coming in were all trying to become Max Perkinses, and that was the last thing we needed in that period of publishing history. We should have been exploring every field of publishing, and the Perkins legacy confined us to *belles lettres*.

The Scribners trade catalogue in 1946 was narrow, narrower in fact than Perkins himself had been; it was much too much focused on fiction. We were top-heavy with novels and we let other types of work atrophy because of our bright young editors who felt obliged to carry the Perkins banner.

The Scribner Building, at Fifth Avenue and Forty-eighth Street, had been functioning virtually unchanged since it opened at that location in 1913. It had an old open-cage elevator with a venerable attendant; you could look down the shaft as you went up. I nicknamed its maker the Fresh Air Elevator Company, after "Amos 'n' Andy," but it was a little grim. Throughout the building were bare cement floors. The library had one of the very few carpets. It was there that Tom Wolfe was reputed to have spent the night reading his publisher's books until he fell asleep on the floor.

As you came off the elevator on the fifth floor, my father's office was around the corner. On the great curved glass windows were faded and torn silk curtains. Against a wall facing you as you got off the elevator were the plaster models, gilded over, of the ornamental heads that adorned the building façade—the great printers: Benjamin Franklin and Gutenberg and Aldus and Caxton. The furniture was all oak and quite magnificent, and the library was paneled.

The fifth floor housed the editorial department. In a cashier's cage Bob Cratchit's successors computed authors' royalties, these being reported in longhand by old ladies and old men who ticked off the number of sales book by book. Dickens would have made a wonderful scene of it.

Perkins sat at his desk in the corner office. Close by was an octogenarian named Charles Dunn, who sat behind a huge, ancient desk and surreptitiously chewed tobacco. In his youth he had been a great pitcher on the Princeton baseball team, and this was the explanation given for his presence at Scribners. We were a staunch Princeton house. Mr. Dunn was unaware of most of our books; he was a "nonacquiring" editor. Yet one twilight discovery of his deserves everlasting credit: he was the first to see the merits of Alan Paton's *Cry, the Beloved Country*, which came in over the transom in 1947. He spotted that manuscript by an unknown South African schoolmaster as something worth following up. About the time Dunn retired, he and two contemporaries had a combined tenure at Scribners of 150 years.

My father's office was originally that of my great-uncle Arthur, my grandfather's younger brother, who died within two years of my grandfather, in 1932. Their eldest brother, John Blair Scribner, had died young in 1879 at age twenty-nine. His widow, Lucy Skidmore Scribner, subsequently retired to Saratoga, New York, where she founded Skidmore College. Next in line was my grandfather Charles, in whose shadow my great-uncle Arthur lived, confined within narrow responsibilities as the man in charge of the manufacturing and warehousing department. My grandfather was the boss. Arthur, toward the end of his life, was president of the company; but my grandfather, in a rather heavy-handed way, would regularly return from retirement and veto his brother's decisions.

Life on the fifth floor was very informal. The poet John Hall Wheelock, a member of the editorial team, had an office just outside my father's. The furnishings were spartan. Cubicles that no tyro editor today would put up with for five minutes were assigned to the senior editors. Still the assemblage was handsome in its simplicity. Hot-water pipes descended from the ceiling without apology. The walls, plain in color and unadorned, formed a fitting backdrop to the handsome oak furniture, the solid bookcases, and the desks that today rank as collectors' items. Louis Auchincloss once said it was the most beautiful set of offices he had ever seen in New York, but no interior decorator would have dared echo the judgment.

By 1946, the company was rather at sixes and sevens. Since Perkins's health was failing, my father brought in some new editors, including Harry Brague and Burroughs Mitchell. After Max's death, Burroughs became James Jones's editor and oversaw the publication of *From Here to Eternity*. There was also a children's book department headed by Alice Dalgliesh, a great editor. I learned much from her, and became fully committed to publishing children's books, even to the extent of writing one myself, entitled *The Devil's Bridge*.

We had a stagnant reference-book department that was languishing for lack of investment. It was in the hands of a gentleman named Carroll Merritt, whose territory was so sacred that he wouldn't let anyone enter his office. I had to wait until he retired before I could make a fresh start in that important field.

All publishing companies had done well during the war. They made money in disgusting amounts, a fact that probably ruined many old houses: it had been too easy to make money when our government bought books by the carload to distribute to the troops. When the war was over, we had a wonderful balance sheet whose contents we quickly dispersed, in vain.

As Roger Burlingame pointed out in 1946 when he wrote the history of Scribners, it was then "the only firm in the English-speaking world to combine under one management every function of book production and distribution, being printers, binders, publishers, wholesale importers and exporters, and finally booksellers." All of this took place in the Scribner Building except the printing and binding. That was done at 311 West Forty-third Street, the headquarters of the Scribner Press.

The press building had also been designed by Ernest Flagg—his Beaux-Arts training did not inhibit him from taking on utilitarian commercial structures. There we did our printing, plate making, typesetting, binding—the entire making of the physical book. But as time went by, it became apparent that such a plant in the middle of New York City was no longer economically sensible. We gave up manufacturing our own books and sold the building. But it still stands today and still spells "Scribner" in colored bricks to drivers approaching the Lincoln Tunnel via Ninth Avenue.

Aside from one little office called the North River Press, which produced books for outside clients, the old plant worked exclusively for Scribners. In its heyday, in the hurly-burly of the press room, people set display type with a composing stick as the Monotypes and Linotypes crackled away. Among the ancient copy editors with green eyeshades reading galley proofs some were masters of erudition; they could correct Greek iota subscripts with one hand and Napoleon's birth year with the other. When we got rid of the printing plant, we lost this venerable force. Outside printers provided no comparable quality of copyediting and for a while our books suffered editorially.

Perkins was totally useless when it came to copyediting or correcting a text. Such details meant very little to him. Consequently, the early editions of books such as Scott Fitzgerald's *The Great Gatsby* were textually corrupt to a nauseating degree. One of my early tasks was to build a staff that could copyedit with the accuracy that readers demand and authors deserve.

The college department was pretty antiquated, had little staff, and lived on its past. The school department, the so-called el-hi, was even worse off. Old employees approaching retirement were unmotivated to do anything new. It was a sorry picture, because at that time a firm with an established name like Scribners could have taken a large share of the booming market. We missed a crucial opportunity after World War II, when Harper's, Harcourt Brace, Random House, and Little, Brown became large and deservedly great firms. Their success came not only from their trade operations but also from their educational publishing. We remained becalmed. What the company needed was a brand-new staff of lively young editors. But I was conservative; I did not want to come in as the young heir apparent and throw a group of old people out of work. In retrospect, I think I was oversensitive to that situation. As Tolstoy observed, young people are often more conservative than their elders.

Possessing so many insights, skills, and talents, Perkins had given a performance that was hard to follow. It would have been hard for Perkins himself, had he lived longer. For years we tried to publish in the Perkins mode, but it was impossible to make a trade publishing house succeed with talented novelists alone. What we needed was a much broader variety of books. We had been too much enthralled by high literature. It wasn't until we decided to break away from the Perkins tradition of pursuing novels and *belles lettres* exclusively that we began to publish more successfully.

Scribners import-export business went back far into the nineteenth century, back into my grandfather's and great-grandfather's day, when Scribners had a London office called Scribner and Welford. Welford was the English partner, and his acquisitions included Renan's *Life of Jesus* and Karl Marx's *Das Kapital*. Any book that my grandfather felt was too risqué for his American list he would publish under the Scribner and Welford imprint and thus dilute his responsibility. (Apropos of Marx's classic, I happened to discover among my grandfather's files his handwritten editorial appraisal—"Not for us.")

By the time I arrived, this import-export business was nearly passé. We had very cordial relations with many English firms that published books on architecture and country houses and fox hunting, but such books had only modest sales in the United States. I doubt that we ever made money on these imports, with one notable exception, Banister Fletcher's *History of Architecture*, which we published through eighteen revised editions.

The Scribner Book Store was, and has remained, one of the landmarks on Fifth Avenue. The bookstore comprised a rare-book department, a children's-book department, and a large general-book department. I promoted the store's buyer, a Russian prince named Igor Kropotkin, to manage the bookstore, and he became a legend in the field.

If you looked at the figures with an auditor's eye, you saw that the bookstore was heavily subsidized by the publishing company. It never made money for the Scribner family, but we kept it going for decades out of sheer pride and joy. We loved the building and we loved having daily contact with the public. The retail space itself was a sublime vision. My eldest son, an art historian, used to call it the Sistine Chapel of bookselling.

My father, who delegated responsibility, had also inherited too many old-timers from his father's generation and, like the firm, he suffered under their regime a good deal. One of them, Whitney Darrow, the father of the famous *New Yorker* cartoonist, ran the trade department. Whitney had been my grandfather's protégé from the time that my grandfather donated the funds to build the Princeton University Press. Whitney was named the press's first director, and was later recruited for Scribners as business manager.

Whitney had a strong personality and much esprit de corps, but he wasn't a book lover. He viewed many of the decisions of the editors—of Max Perkins and Wallace Meyer and John Hall Wheelock—with a censorious eye. They sponsored books of high literary merit that didn't sell well, and to Whitney that was proof that the company wasn't being operated on sound business principles. My father often bristled at Whitney's criticism of Max Perkins, which contributed to the constant strain between the business and the literary sides of publishing. My father had to serve as a reluctant referee.

A gregarious man with Rotary Club camaraderie, Whitney knew everyone in the book business. From these contacts he could see, at least with hindsight, that Scribners was culpably wrong not to take advantage of the opportunities in educational publishing. Unfortunately, his pronounced skepticism about literature in general undermined his credibility. He was so loudly unsympathetic to many of the important literary works we did that his juster criticisms of the firm went unheeded. His lack of competence in literature made him useless as an adviser. For example, he complained that Marcia Davenport's last novel, *The Constant Image*, was a dirty book because it described an extramarital affair in Milan. He thought that Hemingway's *Old Man and the Sea* was just a book about catching a fish; he couldn't understand how it would sell. And when Marjorie Kinnan Rawlings's *The Yearling* was published in 1938, he considered it a juvenile book and thought that it was ridiculous to be publishing it on our adult list.

The rumor was that Whitney's wife, Alice, who had once been his secretary, served as his literary guide; when a book came, Whitney would take it home for Alice to read and report on. If she said, "Gee, this is a great book!" Whitney was full of enthusiasm. The reverse judgement would make him inveigh against the book and its sponsoring editor.

Whitney's last intervention on the fifth-floor scene centered on a very entertaining book, *Journey to the End of an Era*, by a Princeton graduate named Melvin Hall. Hall had taken an automobile trip through the farthermost stretches of the Soviet Union and had written his book in the manner of Negley Farson or John Gunther. It was a very good book, better than we perhaps realized, for we had wrapped it in a lackluster jacket. Just before publication, Whitney wanted to revise the presentation of the book, so we got a new jacket, and we put together a huge advertising budget. It was a lead balloon. *Journey to the End of an Era* was too prosaic a title for a lively adventure story; it sounded like a sociological treatise or a history. Whitney's eleventh-hour intervention was intended to demonstrate his publishing know-how, and it didn't work. It was not entirely his fault, but it was a general disappointment.

Whitney was approaching seventy when I arrived at Scribners; he belonged to my grandfather's era. When I became president of the company in 1952, he had the title of assistant to the president. He may have thought it would give him the authority to make the reforms he believed were needed and that I would simply step out of the way. But I didn't. For years before, he had constantly suggested that my father retire, become chairman of the board, and let Whitney run the company. But my father was too aware of Whitney's insensitivity to the literary side of publishing to comply with his suggestion. Many of our authors were complaining that Whitney cut their advertisements and that his interest in their writing was nil. And occasionally an author would come along with no literary pretensions at all, and Whitney was likely to adopt that author as his pet.

Such was the generational conflict I had stepped into. As my father had left my grandfather's desk untouched, so he tried to leave the structure of the company untouched. I believe that Whitney, who had come from the Princeton Press to Scribners as a relatively young man, engaged in continual conflict even with my grandfather. My grandfather would naturally have felt that Whitney was coming on too strong as a lawgiver in fields beyond his qualifications.

I remember once seeing an interoffice memo that Whitney had sent my grandfather, in which my grandfather had circled the word *I* each time it appeared. It was a constellation of *I*'s followed by verbs of action. Though the circles showed that my grandfather disliked the egotistical, overbearing tone, he would never have asked Whitney to leave—virtually nobody was asked to leave Scribners. That was another tradition I inherited.

By contrast, John Hall Wheelock, who was a poet of great stature, was also a gifted editor and a modest man. He worked on books that cannot have been congenial to him—for example, the romances of Taylor Caldwell, whose work, beginning with *Dynasty of Death* and *The Eagles Gather*, was published by Scribners for a time. As a poet who had been wonderfully educated in this country and in Germany, Wheelock was really overqualified for trade publishing. He was most conscientious but cannot have enjoyed or esteemed some of the literary fare of the day. He was constantly hoping to find best-selling authors, but he didn't have the commercial nose for what the public would like and what makes a publisher succeed.

Wheelock was, quite naturally, our poetry editor. I had worried greatly about the difficulties of publishing poetry and wanted to give it every possible chance at Scribners. I got the idea that instead of publishing small, slim volumes, I would put three hitherto unpublished poets together under one cover and call the series Poets of Today. I asked Wheelock, who was then about to retire, to choose the first three poets. He did so and wrote an introduction to each poet and a general essay on aspects of contemporary poetry. We continued the series for eight years, bringing out twenty-four poets in all. James Dickey and Donald Finkel were among the first. Some of them turned out to be very fine poets. None had been previously published in book form. Some expressed annoyance at having to share the suite with two other poets, though the practical benefit was obvious: one poet's friends and another poet's friends combined to guarantee a larger immediate public for the volumes.

All went well, except for one thing that is terribly embarrassing to confess. Concentrating as I was on getting new poets published, it never occurred to me that some of these poets might prove "best-sellers" in their degree and therefore worth keeping on our list. We had fallen into the appalling policy of not publishing them beyond that first volume. I cannot explain why I was so blind. I was so narrowly intent on this pious enterprise of publishing the new that I forgot my own stake in it, the capture for our list of important writers. James Dickey, for example, went on to be published elsewhere and has had a most successful career as poet and novelist.

Using the same pattern for the short-story genre, I published a series of books called *Short Story 1*, *Short Story 2*, and *Short Story 3*, bringing together the work of three or four promising writers of fiction. I am happy to say that some of those authors we did continue to publish, Gina Berriault for one.

Another gifted and self-effacing editor was Wallace Meyer. It was he who edited Douglas Southall Freeman, whose multivolume *Robert E. Lee* and *Lee's Lieutenants* continue in print a half century after their original publication.

A third on our top staff, Burroughs Mitchell, was an enormous admirer of Perkins. Eager and hard-working, he would take on all kinds of projects. He even edited a cookbook at one point, although his real interests were literary and he made many friends among authors and their agents. He was rather bolder than his colleagues and sought out some of the more uninhibited writers of his generation. But that caused no friction with his fellows, Jack Wheelock and

Wallace Meyer; Mitchell was a pleasant person to work with. He came to Scribners about the same time I did. He brought to us Morton Thompson, who wrote *Not as a Stranger*, a big best-seller, and Gerald Green, author of *The Last Angry Man*.

But his greatest success and most enduring affiliation was with James Jones. Perkins had read some of James Jones's first drafts of *From Here to Eternity* and had made some sensible suggestions. The book needed a lot of work, and Burroughs became to James Jones what Perkins had been to Thomas Wolfe.

In those days—the late forties and fifties—books came to us in several ways. Sometimes one of our authors recommended them; sometimes people came in cold. James Jones was one of the latter. Alan Paton was sent to us by a man named Aubrey Burns with whom Paton had been staying out on the West Coast. Many authors sent in their work because of the reputation of the firm and the kind of books that we published.

But the time had come when almost every author had to have an agent. Both Burroughs Mitchell and Harry Brague had many good agent connections, but Scribners was not noted for being agent-oriented, probably because its successful policies were set in an era of publishing when agents played a much smaller role. This relative neglect of the need for good contacts with agents became a drawback to the firm. We were—and regrettably I must include myself—rather snooty about having to bend to the demands of agents.

Burroughs understood our dilemma. He reported that other people in the industry did not know where Scribners got its books. Perhaps they thought we grew them in the cellar like mushrooms; certainly we weren't active in the thoroughfares of the contemporary book trade. We regarded our writers as family. Occasionally an editor paid advances out of his own pocket, as Perkins had often done. The firm had an anxious sense of the importance of the editor's role.

Agents trooped into our lives as the business became increasingly commercial. Movie contracts, magazine serialization, and foreign rights automatically brought agents in. Today agents play a role—sometimes an adversarial role, to my way of thinking—that dominates trade publishing. They often benefit from breaking up many a happy marriage between publisher and author. They occasionally act more as match-breakers than matchmakers. The emphasis on advances and "front money" feeds the temptation to auction off the author's next book and raise the ante, rather than rely on a long-term relationship to produce, in the end, greater revenues for both.

The loyal feeling of mutual obligation between author and publisher that was so prevalent in the early years of our history has not been entirely extinguished, by any means. We still enjoy many strong attachments of the former kind.

Perkins's rooted dislike of books that were not fiction was one of the problems I eventually had to face. Wallace Meyer was editing the solid histories of Douglas Southall Freeman, but if Perkins liked anything other than novels it was quirky books, such as *The Dyer's Hand*, which dealt with Shakespeare's "true identity." He also favored newsworthy books, such as Kravchenko's *I Chose Freedom* and Bullitt's *The Great Globe Itself*. But he had no use for books on practical subjects or serious studies in the various departments of thought. His eyes would glaze over a book on physics, but he seemed fascinated by pseudoscience. He would say, "We really have to consider this one seriously, because though it sounds crazy, the man may be right. So it's our obligation to bring his book out."

In his own area, William Savage, our editor of religious books, made all the decisions. His adviser was Reinhold Niebuhr, by then one of the most famous professors at the Union Theological Seminary, and between them they put together the finest list of books on religion ever assembled by any publisher—a virtual tour de force. Niebuhr was completely nonsectarian. He brought us the neo-Thomism of Jacques Maritain side by side with the profoundly Protestant views of Paul Tillich. He covered the spectrum of theological conviction in the most marvelously objective way, all the while writing his many books for our imprint.

Somewhere in the shuffle—it pains me physically to record it—Bill Savage got the idea that Niebuhr had fulfilled his mission and was no longer needed in his advisory role. Niebuhr must have been puzzled, but being such a big mind, he was not offended. He continued to write new books for us. It shows the naïve decentralization of Scribners that Bill Savage could have severed such a beneficial tie without ever consulting me.

Before Alice Dalgliesh became head of the children's-book department, this side of our publishing had not been differentiated from the adult trade department. Her original task had been to edit for the educational department more lively books in social studies for elementary schools. When Alice arrived, Scribners employed no women except as secretaries. When she came to my father and asked him to give her an office, he replied, "Oh, do you really need one?" That was my father: pleasantly oblivious of dawning realities. But Alice got her office, and an assistant, pronto.

She was a professional through and through. Indeed, she gave me my real education in publishing as a business, as a set of obligations, and as a career requiring the highest standards. She felt that she had a *calling* to be a children's-book editor and that her books had to be of the highest possible quality. She scorned the sappy and sentimental. Although she condescended to publish new editions of *Peter Pan*, she thought some of Barrie's stories were deplorable.

Sometimes I could kid Alice into publishing a book I liked, but she would make clear that "I'm doing this because Charlie likes it." Besides humor and good humor, she had the eager curiosity of a young person. And she was eclectic in her tastes; for example, she took on Alfred Morgan's books on steam engines and electricity, which in those days were labeled "for boys." She hired true artists, and many of the books that she published were books *by* artists, with an added story—a libretto, so to speak—to carry the art along. She herself wrote books. One, entitled *The Silver Pencil*, published as a children's book, was about being a writer, and it was her own story. Her *Bears on Hemlock Mountain* and *Courage of Sarah Noble* became small classics of children's literature. As a colleague and close friend, it was wonderful to watch her at work.

After the Second World War, school systems all over the country were buying library books, and Alice's list was aimed directly at this very profitable market. All the people involved—the editors, the artists, the reviewers, the teachers, the school librarians—shared a common resolve to give American youngsters the best literature that could be got. Clearly, during my apprentice period one of the few things that I got right was to realize how important Alice was to the firm and to give her everything she wanted. I put up with daily scoldings and resignations to keep her on the team. When she finally retired, I had a difficult time finding someone fit to take her place.

Marjorie Kinnan Rawlings had written a children's book called *The Secret River*, which we decided to publish in 1955, two years after her death. Set in the South, it was about a little girl whose mother was a hairdresser. It was not made clear whether the girl was supposed to be black or white, and we were a little troubled by this ambiguity. Whatever our decision, we could land on the wrong side of the school boards. Then I had an inspiration. I had the entire book printed in black ink on brown paper, so there was no imputed color in the illustrations. That was one of my silent contributions to dissolving the color barrier in the 1950s.

Children's-book editors were our first women editors; the first in our adult trade department was Elinor Parker. She had been manager of the Scribner Book Store, and she proved to be another splendid recruit. Nowadays there are at least as many women in publishing as men—perhaps more; the postwar years were the period of transition. Having just come out of the navy and worked with Waves, I knew firsthand that women were as well qualified as men for any intellectual task. But for many, the changed outlook seemed a break with venerable publishing tradition. It was a break that served us especially well.

When we published Alan Paton's *Cry, the Beloved Country* in 1948, I wanted an ad that would do it justice. I toiled and wrote and rewrote to find the right headline. It so happened that nobody at Scribners had thought much about this extraordinary novel; no one could help me—it had been released absentmindedly, so to speak. But it received wonderful reviews. Orville Prescott in *The New York Times* said it was one of the great books, period. That would be quoted first but what to put "above" it? After hours in pursuit of inspiration, I came up with the phrase "A Spontaneous Chorus of Praise"—such was my single contribution to book advertising. Yet I confess I felt flattered when the Book-of-the-Month Club used that headline in announcing *Cry, the Beloved Country* to its members.

Advertising and marketing in those days were rather amateurish. I, who knew nothing, was in charge. I had a young woman to help me write the publicity, but many, if not most, of the jacket flaps were my own work. I also wrote the copy for the ads, most of which, I must say in all modesty, were painfully bad. I remember writing jacket flaps for all kinds of books I hadn't read. We prepared our own layouts in-house and beautiful they were. I mean to say they were grim.

We spent tons of money on advertising. Like most publishing companies we had made a great deal of money during the war, and we were now spending it advertising in *The New York Times*, daily and Sundays, and in such magazines as *Harper's* and *The Atlantic*. We advertised in and out of town. Our cut-rate agent placed the ads, but as he wasn't paid a regular salary, he couldn't help us on the creative side; he just helped us spend the money.

Scribners catalogues in 1946 were austere—no charm at all in the presentation of our books. It was a holdover from an earlier day when catalogues were not a selling tool but simply lists. Ours, which included the extensive backlist, were about as inviting as a telephone book. We did have seasonal catalogues with color, but they, too, were rather drab.

One of my first concerns was to try to bring back to life our rich backlist, all the way up, from Robert Louis Stevenson to Hemingway. That put me in the business of revising as well as rewriting the catalogues. It was perhaps foolish on my part to do many of these tasks myself, instead of assigning them to others. In retrospect, I wish I had spent more time on issues that were more crucial.

Books were sold, then as now, by salesmen who visit the retail bookstores and also through wholesale jobbers. The sales force was small. We had no more than six or seven men. They came each season to a so-called sales conference, which took place in a tiny little room and was presided over by Max Perkins. Nobody else was allowed in, not even the editors who had acquired the new books on the list. Nowadays a sales conference resembles a Passion play: everybody is invited to participate and marvel at the drama. In Perkins's time, it was all done *in camera*. A skeptical group of salesmen gathered about him, and the editor-in-chief would say: "Now, here's a book by Robert Briffault. I really don't know why we ever took that book. It's a curious book, and it's got some very embarrassing chapters"—or words to that effect. I am not joking: that was the sales pitch for the book—informal to the point of being Pickwickian. How in God's name was a salesman supposed to sell the work? Whitney Darrow himself was not allowed to come to the sales conference, though he was head of the whole sales operation. It was incredible.

Somehow the books got sold. The firm did get to know something of Perkins's quirky presentations—his often quite irrelevant opening remark, followed (if he thought the book was really good) by something more to the point. His favorable opinions would filter down through the usual channels of office rumor. I should add that one of our salesmen in the college department, Perry Knowlton, later became a trade editor and eventually a leading literary agent.

Although we were doing our share of publishing history and biography, we were still very much a fiction and *belles lettres* firm; I doubt whether we ever lost that image entirely. But we were, I repeat, "literary" to excess. Our failure to capitalize on important genres that we were *deliberately* missing was due to the strength of the Perkins tradition. That neglect put us, a relatively small company, into head-on collision with almost all the major publishing houses—Harper's, Simon & Schuster, Random House, and Doubleday.

They had far greater means for getting good books. The agents went to them before they came to us. If we had not diversified away from fiction, which is dominated by the agents, we would probably have languished to the danger point. Part of our success in continuing as a private company was to stop relying on trade books alone.

During the fifties, a man named Norman Snow took over Whitney's job; but, regrettably, many of the conflicts between editor and business manager persisted. The man who daily sees the business side of publishing thinks that the editors are numskulls who know nothing about money. The editors think that the business head is a yahoo who knows nothing about books. Probably every firm is plagued in the same way. The business mind never understands that literary judgment takes imagination and flair. Even more important, the business mind never learns that best-sellers are not predictable. With similar prejudices, the salesman feels most comfortable with a book that has been acclaimed as a best-seller before publication. The truth is that business risks taken on the basis of experienced intuition alone oftentimes pay off handsomely. That is one of the most interesting features of publishing.

When I joined Scribners, we were high in reputation and low in performance and profitability. But by the early fifties we had acquired an encouraging list. It included Charles Lindbergh's *The Spirit of St. Louis*, Alan Paton's *Too Late the Phalarope*, Gerald Green's *The Last Angry Man*, and Morton Thompson's *Not as a Stranger*. Bennett Cerf of Random House wrote, "Isn't it wonderful to see a fine old house just come out with smash best-sellers?"

It was a gracious accolade, but in his phrase "fine old house" lay the implication that we were old-fashioned, not really in the swim. The unspoken conclusion was that we had passed our peak. If so, what was to be done? Today the publishing marketplace is dominated by Hollywood, by the agents, and by the sale of subsidiary rights. All that which was in embryo when my father entered the business is now preponderant. To my grandfather the book business today would be unrecognizable. It belongs to the entertainment industry much more than to the literary world. You can see it in the bookstore chains. I recently went into one of the chain stores on Fifth Avenue and asked for that obscure classic, *A Tale of Two Cities*; the sales clerk had never heard of it. In the heyday of the Scribner Book Store the clerks all were, if not men or women of letters, lettered men and women. They knew what had been and was being published; they lived in a literary environment.

Mine was thus a time of change—of difficult changes—of generations, of rapid and extensive upheavals in the marketplace, in American life, in taste and literature. Added to these in publishing per se came the fundamental change brought by the paperback revolution. But that is for another chapter.

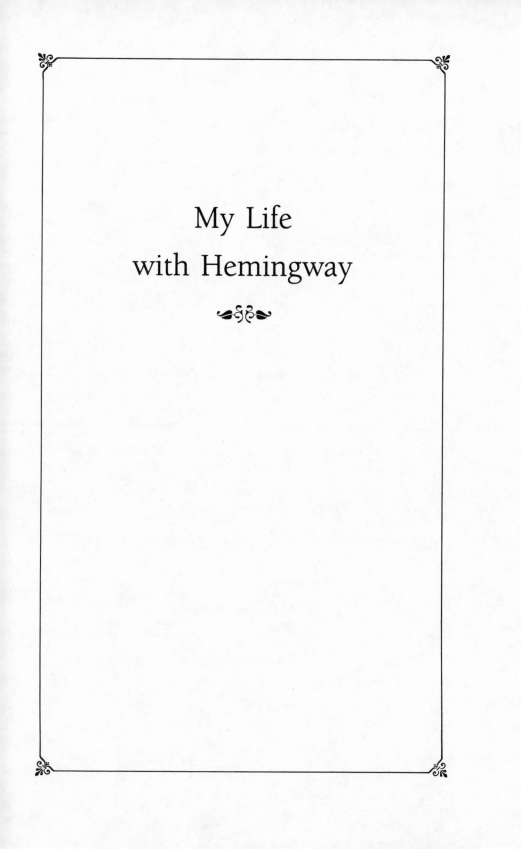

My Life
with Hemingway

As I mentioned earlier, one of my first assignments at Scribners in 1946 was to edit a new edition of Hemingway's *A Farewell to Arms*. I had never copyedited a book before. Here was a new edition, newly set, and somebody had to read proof to make sure there were no typos. Nobody showed me how to read proof, but I read, and checked, and tried to catch the howlers.

I also was to write to Hemingway to tell him he had to send a preface for this illustrated edition. Hemingway had not liked the illustrations; that is why they asked *me* to write to him. My father and Perkins were afraid that if either of them wrote the letter, Hemingway would blow up; by sending me in as cannon fodder, if Hemingway blew up, the fire could be contained.

So I wrote to Hemingway, asking, "Will you give us a new preface?" He wrote back the most charming letter anybody has ever received. It was very funny; and it was very kind, because he was trying to put me on the footing of camaraderie that my father had with him. This established between us a connection that was of great importance when my father died. But at the time the notion that I should be the one to write to an author who was my father's closest friend seemed absurd. Despite Hemingway's grumbling, the edition of *A Farewell to Arms* went through. It was a lovely edition, illustrated by Rasmusson, but Hemingway never liked it.

When I corresponded with him a couple of years later, he wrote at one point and said he hoped we were "building up a young ball team." That was typical of Hemingway. He loved to get some athletic figure of speech into what he was saying. Once I wrote him that my son Charlie, then a year and a half old, was taking all the books out of our bookcases in our New York apartment. Hemingway replied, "Well, he's just getting all the deadwood out of your company."

I wrote to him on another occasion, saying, "My children don't think I'm very smart. But I told them, how come if I'm as dumb as you think, that I'm making all the money for this family?" Hemingway loved it. He wrote back, "That's what I'm going to tell my children." Hemingway had a perfected gallows humor; he liked rough jokes, with a sting at the end. He once gave me some rules for life, among them: "Always do sober what you said you'd do when you were drunk. That will teach you to keep your mouth shut!" Once we sent him a package at the Finca Vigía, which he acknowledged by writing: "I've just gotten a third notice from the Cuban post office that something is waiting for me down there. Actually, it's the first notice, but they've just run out of them, so they used the third notice."

My father used to let me read what Ernest wrote to him. In Hemingway's letters to me after my father died, he always referred to him as having been his best friend. My father certainly loved his author friend's utterly charming letters. They were all written in his rolling handwriting, the envelope covered with Cuban postage stamps. We knew what fun we could expect when one of those envelopes arrived. In these letters he would test out little things, such as the incident of Scott Fitzgerald's fear about his sexual anatomy, later included (over my strenuous objections) in *A Moveable Feast*. In writing down his doubts, he was hoping to get a response, yes or no. These trial balloons would often come out later in his books. My father's affection for Hemingway was deep. They were near contemporaries and they had great fun insulting each other—what Hemingway liked to call "joking rough."

After my father died, I made a tremendous effort to bring Hemingway's books back into print in a comprehensive set of our own. I terminated licenses that meant a lot to him sentimentally, such as those to Modern Library editions. The Modern Library had been part of his growing up, as it was for so many of us, but I decided to take back all the books we had farmed out in paperback or in any kind of derivative edition. I made a list of them and wrote to Hemingway, "I can get you higher royalties if you let me take all these books back from the reprinters and let me sell them directly. I know you'll make more money."

Hemingway liked the idea: "Okay, if you wish." In his reply he went on to give his verdict for the reissue of every book. He didn't just say yes, yes, yes. He had a different answer, a different phrase for each one, although the answers were uniformly affirmative ("if you wish," "if you have to," etc.), which I found amusing. It seemed as if he did not want to miss the opportunity of writing something different; nor did he disguise his regret at allowing the Modern Library licenses to be withdrawn.

It was then that his income really began to soar. It was about the time we were publishing *The Old Man and the Sea*, and he was making almost as much money a month as he had made in any recent year. He expressed his appreciation for my taking the steps that led to so sizable an increase in his income.

Throughout his correspondence with my father, Hemingway kept asking for "loans." He didn't want to call them advances. They *were* advances, but as they were not tied to any particular book, they were to be considered loans. Every other author in New York was asking for advances against the royalties of a new book, and Ernest could have got any amount he wanted on any of them. He preferred these loans and was proud of the distinction. He thought of himself as not like other authors, who boasted of their advances: his publisher trusted him with loans.

When he sent me the first chapters of what we later called *A Moveable Feast* (it was Mary Hemingway who thought up that title), he gave the manuscript to A. E. Hotchner, his jack-of-all-trades, to hand over to us. I thought these chapters first-rate. I called Ernest, and he sounded like a seventeen-year-old author who had never had anything published: "Oh, you liked them? I *thought* you might be willing to lend me money on the basis of them." It was touching, this dealing with the boyish Ernest. It was a measure of his insecurity after a long black period that a positive report from his publisher could please him so.

At an earlier moment during an unproductive phase, he turned out *Across the River and into the Trees*, a pretty weak novel. In it, he had included the most horrendous, insulting references to his third wife, Martha Gellhorn. They were beyond the pale, and my father wheedled him very diplomatically into taking out this and then that and the other. I doubt that Hemingway would have agreed to it for anyone else. He did it for my father because he never thought of my father as a literary person. Had my father been some famous man of letters, Hemingway would have resisted, but he could not feel rebuked by the suggestions of a businessman.

Hemingway's close relations with my father, as of boyhood pals, was the cause of his great friendliness toward me. But I made a conscious decision not to try to be his friend in that same way at all. I was going to keep our dealings professional and not call him Papa. I did call him Ernest, but I never was one of the court that surrounded him in later life. It would have been trading on my father's credit and Hemingway's good nature.

So I kept my distance; virtually all my letters to Ernest were about business matters. He asked me once to come down to Cuba, but I declined. I think my guardian angel was doing me a good turn, because I suspect that if I had ever been on a social footing with Ernest, the happy relationship would not have lasted. He tried to draw me into his circle, but I quietly resisted.

He wrote to my father in 1949 apropos of my engagement: "Please tell young Charlie we will not be able to come to his wedding. We'll be glad to pay for and inscribe any of the larger books, if you send them down here." He followed this up with a note: "Think young Charlie makes a mistake not to have some of those aged books for doorstops." The reason for this postscript was that my father was not well at the time—it was not long before his death—and he must have forgotten to mention the offer to me. Worse than that, when I got married, my family, by the grossest carelessness, forgot to include Ernest's wife Mary in the wedding invitation. Hemingway was furious.

My father had suffered for years from an enlarged heart and an aneurysm of the aorta. His death in 1952 was instantaneous when the artery burst. Hemingway wrote me a beautiful condolence letter in which he added a postscript to explain that he was addressing me as a civilian only because he didn't know my rank: it was classic Hemingway, who paid close attention to military ranks. It was so thoughtful a letter and revealed a little-known side of the man. It deserves to be reprinted in its entirety:

Dear Charlie:

It would seem strange to call your father Charlie and then address you as Mr. Scribner. But I can do it if you would prefer and if it makes things any simpler.

Please know how badly I felt to be away and out of touch when your father died. We must have left the harbor about an hour before he felt ill from what Wallace Meyer and [Alfred] Rice wrote me and Mary brought word of his death the following Saturday evening. From down the coast we tried to write your mother how Mary and I felt about him. But I do not even know if she received the letter as it had to be sent inland to be posted.

I won't try to write to you how much he meant to me as a friend and as a publisher. He was the best and closest friend that I had and it seems impossible that I will never have another letter from him. It does not do any good to talk about it and there is nothing to say that makes it any easier. Since he had to die at least he has gotten it over with.

If there is anything practical I can do please let me know. After the March 15 income tax has been paid I will plan to draw nothing more on my loan account this year except for the four payments of $750 that Rice figures must be made against 1952 tax. Please cancel the monthly payment of $100 a month to Gregory Hemingway as of March First ie. make no payment on March First nor thereafter. As soon as the money is paid me for the cinema rights to Across The River and Into the Trees I will pay something to reduce my loan account. There is $25,000 in escrow as an advance against ten percent of the gross in that picture deal. But the picture people still have to fulfill certain requirements before it is paid. When I talked to Rice on the phone he was optimistic about them raising all their money. This is the first time he has been optimistic and told me this is the type of deal that cannot be hurried. It is a good property and there is no sense in making a forced sale when it is possible to wait.

I will try and not worry you about finances nor about anything else. You don't have to write me letters nor have me on your mind in any way. I know what a terribly tough job you have now with Navy, Estate and the House of Scribner to look after. They shouldn't do that to any human being. Please take it as easy as you can and feel free to call on me in any way that I can be of help. If there is anything Mary and I can do for your Mother please let us know. She likes Mary and she likes the sea and to fish and she might like to come down some time and stay with us and get some fishing with Mary.

I plan to pick up the vacation where we left it and not worry about anything nor think of things that can't be helped and keep on getting in the best of shape to hit the book again. On the boat we were getting to bed at nine, sleeping well, getting up at daylight and fishing all forenoon and reading and loafing in the afternoon. I could feel the batteries rechargeing every day. It is not fair to *anyone* not to keep in shape to do your best work and I am going to get in the best shape I can now no matter what other things have to [take] second priority for the necessary time. I've over-worked for 18 months.

This is not a good letter, Charlie. But I still feel too sad to write a good one.

Your friend
Ernest Hemingway

Am sorry I don't know your rank so address this as a civilian.

EH

Before I went back into the service during the Korean War, someone at Scribners relicensed the short story "The Snows of Kilimanjaro" to *Esquire* for a one hundred dollars. That rankled in Hemingway's mind for months and months, he was so angry. He considered that it was very likely the best story he had ever written, and he thought he should have been paid at least a thousand dollars, if not more. In his private thought, "Some jerk at Scribners had given it away for nothing." I don't know who blundered, but it was truly unforgivable. When something of the sort happened to him, Ernest kept coming back to it again and again. When one of his lawyers once made a mistake at his expense, he said, "It's like having a pet cobra in the house to bite me once each day." At other times the image was "It's like having a spastic outfielder." He never was at a loss for virulent words of denunciation.

At one point, Bennett Cerf wrote Scribners a letter presumably aimed at luring Hemingway away from us, or at least at getting him back into the Modern Library. It was a very tricky letter, very subtle, and it had to be answered with care. Hemingway approved my reply: "I'm glad the way you got through that mine field." His loyalty to us was cast iron.

Not that I blamed Cerf. He had been selling Hemingway's fiction for years, and my policy of taking it all back was cruel and unusual punishment. *The Sun Also Rises* and the short stories were at the heart of the modern section of the Modern Library collection. I knew this, having educated myself by reading virtually right through the series. But my obligation to do all I could for our authors—and the firm—justified my policy, as did also the practical results I mentioned earlier.

The situation before I intervened deserves a word more. Whitney Darrow had the responsibility of selling subsidiary rights, and as he had no real faith in books, he put a low value on our backlist. Those authors Perkins liked were in his view unstable, unproductive types, so that any time Whitney could get fifty or a hundred dollars for a subsidiary right on one of their books, he considered it a stroke of luck. In this mood, he had Hemingway licensed to Bantam Books, Pocket Books, and the New American Library, as well as Viking and the Modern Library. Whitney was scraping together a few dollars whenever he could.

As a result, most of Hemingway was not available in our original editions in hardcover. Logically considered, we were no longer Hemingway's main publishers. That was the state of affairs I felt compelled to turn around. I disliked paperbacks anyway and wanted to see Hemingway restored to hardcover, full size, and good paper and print.

In time, we came to see that there would be still greater advantage in publishing all the backlist works of Fitzgerald, Alan Paton, and Marjorie Kinnan Rawlings in paperback, and I converted them to that form to make up a sizable paperback line. I could not have done it without their being rescued from others first. I did the same with other Scribners authors, bringing back Galsworthy in toto when "Masterpiece Theatre" presented *The Forsyte Saga* in 1970. It turned out to have been the perfect strategy.

In January 1950, Lillian Ross did a steadily sarcastic profile of Hemingway for *The New Yorker*. Hemingway was depicted as talking his "Indian" talk—how he could knock anybody out of the ring except Shakespeare. He opined that he probably could not beat Tolstoy, but might be able to survive a couple of rounds with him. It was idiotic, but Hemingway seemed to be basking in the limelight and allowing the interviewer to make a fool of him. She was clearly intent on doing just that, all in the presence of my father, sitting quietly like the modest man he was. In Lillian Ross's article, whenever anything significant was said, my father was rebuffed as saying something like "Yuh, yuh, yuh, yah," which was his unfortunate stammer. He was very shy and stammered when asked any question.

To make matters worse, he didn't know who Lillian Ross was. He may have thought she was a stenographer taking down answers to prepared questions. Though I never admitted his error to anybody, I felt very bitter about the way she pilloried my father. On his side, he made scathing comments about her that I have kept—and intend to keep—to myself. It was a sorry episode.

In September 1950, Hemingway wrote to my father "So sorry about young Charlie." I had been drafted back into military service, and it was hard for my father, because he was not well and counted on me to help him more and more in the company. Selfishly, I didn't try not to go. America was at war in Korea and I felt I could contribute useful work as a cryptanalyst. Hemingway, of course, never would think that being called up in itself was a calamity. But under the circumstances, it *was* a calamity for my father.

When my father died, the firm made a request to the navy for my release. For a while I commuted between Washington and New York, and finally I got my discharge. In Hemingway's first letter after my return, reprinted earlier, he said, "It would seem strange to call your father Charlie and then address you as Mr. Scribner. But I can do it if you would prefer . . ."—characteristic Hemingway in its blend of humor and courtesy. How could I say, "Please don't call me Charlie?" As I said, I never called him Papa. It would have been both fawning and presumptuous, trying to qualify as a new intimate. I think he liked the fact that I didn't. He hated the name Ernest—he thought it was a stuffy, Victorian name—but that was his name and I always wrote "Dear Ernest."

I had to set the tone of our relations, neither acting standoffish nor polishing the apple. Hemingway, I knew, loved professionalism, whether in a writer or a bullfighter. He admired people who had a trade and stuck to it. That decided me: I would be a professional publisher.

When for some reason Hemingway was on the warpath, he could be formidable. Once, he left some fishing rods in the care of Maxwell Perkins, and somehow the tip of one got broken. Hemingway made it a *casus belli*. Perkins must have been careless, he could never be forgiven. Perkins had to talk fast against Hemingway's fury. Another time Ernest left some shotgun shells in the vaults of the Scribners printing plant, and we had to cope with that. The shells had dried out: firing *one* would take your shoulder off; the stockpile was as reassuring as a live hand-grenade. Life with Ernest was not easy.

In November 1952, Mary Hemingway came to New York and I met her for the first time. She came alone. It was about then that Hemingway had sold to *Life* magazine, through Leland Hayward, *The Old Man and the Sea*. The one-shot serialization was to precede book publication by Scribners, and publishers and well-wishers thought that it was a disaster for us to be scooped by a magazine. But there was nothing to do. When Mary came to visit us at home, at 31 East Seventy-ninth Street, she was obviously feeling a little guilty about the *Life* prepublication. I took the view that it was nothing to shed tears about. In a couple of years, nobody would remember—or care. The sale to *Life* made a great deal of money for Hemingway when he needed it badly.

In book form, *The Old Man and the Sea* sold like blazes. It hit a level that has never come down since; it is selling at a best-seller rate today. After the first rush, when we began The Scribner Library, our trade paperback line, we sold innumerable copies to schools as it became a contemporary high school classic. Thus began Hemingway's emergence from a slough of low earnings into the class of high-income writers. The same happened for Scott Fitzgerald and for all those classic Scribners authors whose works I recovered from other paperback lines—and put into our own. I should add that on ours we paid the author full royalties. It was most satisfactory.

The enormous success of *The Old Man and the Sea* did not change Hemingway except for a certain glow he ever after felt about it. In that period he was doubtless working on books that I published many years after his death. I can't help wondering what will happen if we meet in an afterlife. He may be so angry at me for doing this that if killing is still possible, he will kill me. But I've thought up a good excuse. If he says, "Why did you publish my letters when you knew I didn't want my letters published? Why did you publish books I never finished?," I will say: "Look, before you died you told me you had safe-deposit boxes full of manuscripts that were going to earn good royalties for your family. I was the person best able to bring out those books, posthumously, and they *have* done well for your family. I merely made good your boast."

Hemingway reassured me about *The Old Man and the Sea* by arguing that the *Life* publication wouldn't affect sales because the people who read *Life* aren't the people who read books, and the people who read books will buy the book anyway. It proved a good argument—and a sensational publication. James Michener had been instrumental in recommending it to *Life*, the story having made a tremendous impact on him. *The Old Man and the Sea* is indeed a splendid novella, but its effect on Hemingway's career was surely disproportionate to the importance of the work itself.

In 1954, Hemingway won the Nobel Prize for Literature. He most graciously wrote to me, "It would be impossible to have a sounder friend or adviser than you have been." The prize meant a great deal to him, like the success of his novella in *Life* and as a book. The joint event, so to speak, rescued him from his low fortunes and low self-esteem. He called up General Charles ("Buck") Lanham, who was a great friend and a great hero in World War II, and said, "I've got it. I got that thing." Lanham probably asked, "What thing?" To which Hemingway replied, "The big one," or "The Nobel thing," or some such words. He was very, very happy.

For quite a while, he had been not at all well. He was an old man before his time. He was then much younger than I am now, but he had aged rapidly. Once or twice during his last years, I met him in an apartment he had rented on Fifth Avenue and Sixty-second Street. He was failing visibly. He seemed almost frail; his arms weren't the old burly limbs. He was tentative in his movements and uncommonly shy. Somebody else has remarked on this that it was a shyness compounded with egotism, shyness being from the start an integral part of his ego.

About that time, I went to see Ernest with our senior editor, Harry Brague, who had had a hand in editing him. We were asking him to decide what he wanted published first, the pieces on Paris that later made up *A Moveable Feast* or a huge mass of material on Spain and bullfighting that would have to be cut drastically. Hemingway was not willing to cut, because (he said) the Proustian detail of the bullfights was essential. To me, at least, it seemed that one account of a bullfight (or at most two) resembled all the rest; so we had quite a job of persuasion ahead of us.

Hemingway proved querulous. He said his eyes were in poor shape—how could he work at anything? And how would he ever be able to shoot anymore? Would he have to learn to shoot by ear? It was a steady stream of self-scarifying. We finally agreed that he would do the Paris pieces.

Brague and I were for the time being coeditors for Hemingway. After our visit Brague said, "I think he isn't happy at the thought of doing the Paris pieces first. Maybe you ought to call him and find out."

I did and it was one of the worst mistakes of my publishing career. Having said, "Ernest, I didn't mean to talk you into this," I went on: "If you'd rather do it the other way. . . ." Now the one thing he did not want at that juncture was even a modicum of uncertainty. He went into a tailspin. I learned subsequently that he said to Aaron Hotchner, "I'm being published by the anchor publishing company, and they are dragging me to the bottom of the ocean." Hotchner was going to put the remark in his book *Papa Hemingway*, but Bennett Cerf very kindly suggested that that reference to us be left out.

The experience made me more cautious. I knew it was all my fault; I had been psychologically blind not to recognize that what he didn't want was any kind of iffyness about what would happen next. He wanted me decisive and telling him what to do. Ernest could not stand uncertainty, could not stand a plan becoming a problem. He did not want to cope with problems. My blunder earned the penalty of good intentions misplaced.

It is an interesting sidelight on Hemingway's mind—as it was a good lesson to me—that the only cure for his awkward willful moods was to let them cool off, evaporate. If, perversely, he didn't want a choice, so be it. It's part of the psychology of being an author. You want some direction.

You want to be told, "This is right and that is wrong," even if you're Hemingway.

Later I was happy to learn that I had not forfeited his trust. I went up to his apartment again and after we had chatted a little, Hemingway said, "Have you any place you can lock something up in your office?" I said, "Sure. I can put it in a filing cabinet and lock the cabinet."

"I want you to take this valise down to Scribners and put it in that filing cabinet of yours."

I said I would, and he went on: "Now, don't lose it, my will is in there." I assured him I would not lose it and, a little embarrassed, added a childish remark: "If I lose it, I'll shoot myself." To which he made a typical Hemingway rejoinder: "That wouldn't do me any good."

I practically chained the valise to my wrist, took a taxi, and got it down to the office. The next morning or the one after that, in came Ernest and said he wanted to look something up in the valise. The cabinet was just outside my door; I unlocked it and sat in my office until he was through rummaging around in his belongings. I knew perfectly well he just wanted to make sure I hadn't lost his valuables. Everything was in order, so he came back in, filled with joyful reassurance—or at least good cheer. At first we stood and talked together; then he sat down in my desk chair. That put me off my stride a little bit; I felt somewhat out of place in my own place. But I asked him if he wanted coffee, and when it came, "With cream?" and "How much?" He said, "Just enough to change the color." Typical, again: Not for him the usual, "Not too much" or "I'll say when." I think that was the last time I saw him.

When he died, Horace Manges, of Weil, Gotshal & Manges, a close personal friend as well as corporate attorney, came to advise me what to do. I told him I had the will in my filing cabinet. We called Alfred Rice, Hemingway's lawyer, to open the will with us. Out came the battered valise and the two lawyers searched through it. They finally saw what might be a will. I was amused to note that each man held on to a part of the paper in such a way that the other couldn't wrench it out of his hand. They had joint possession and nobody present could do any sleight of hand.

Somehow, Alfred Rice got a clear look at it, heaved a sigh of relief, and said, "He's left everything to Mary." They took it away for probate and about a week or so later the will, a holograph drawn up without benefit of lawyers, appeared in the second section of *The New York Times*.

Hemingway was expert enough for his purpose. He bought a form for the introductory language, wrote out the rest longhand, and the thing, with the needed witnesses, proved perfectly adequate legally. Like everything Hemingway did, it was a colorful piece of work. Scribners was proud to have had his confidence, expressed and made evident in this series of incidents.

But his decline during those last years was painful. He went to the Mayo Clinic and had shock treatment for his profound depression; but it brought about no change. He tried repeatedly to kill himself. On one trip from his home in Ketchum, Idaho, to the hospital, he started to walk into the moving propeller of the plane. He was bent on suicide.

I did not dream of urging him to write anything; I only wanted him to get well again and be in good spirits. It was a personal sorrow to know that this giant of a man was played out. A friend of mine wrote a piece on fishing in the Yellowstone, and I sent it to Ernest. He liked it and asked that I send it to his son Jack, who, he said, was a better fisherman than he was.

That was one of the last letters I got from him. There was a little boy in the hospital who was dying, and Ernest wrote him a tender little note, saying, "We'll have to get well, and you and I will go out fishing." The note is included in the volume of his collected letters. It moved me particularly because tenderness was a true part of his character, though not the most visible or best-known side of him.

I think that in his suicidal urge there was a hereditary as well as a psychological component. He knew, of course, that his father had committed suicide. That must have exerted a permanent psychological pressure, and if his intense depression had a genetic source, he succumbed under a double burden.

Soon after his death, I made an office in our building available to Mary so that she could go through his effects and his papers. It was an avalanche, because he was an inveterate paper-saver. And the papers were filled with insects, having been stored in Cuba. I was a little worried that there might be an infestation of Cuban fleas or other bugs all over our building, but we escaped.

The first book we published posthumously was the one I had discussed with him shortly before his death, the Paris pieces, *A Moveable Feast*. It was a great success he didn't live to see. We worked with Mary on the text, because at times he repeated himself over and over. In the one about the pilot fish, for example, Harry Brague and I knew that the intolerable redundancy ought to be cut, and we cut. Hemingway's biographer Carlos Baker scolded me for it. He thought it was immoral to tamper with an author's writing no matter how he had left it. But then it would not have been publishable—or if published, readers would have found those passages a discredit to his memory. We had to do a great deal of the same editing on the several posthumous works that we published later.

The next was *Byline*. This was a group of pieces from the *Toronto Star*, not protected by American copyright. An editor named Hanrahan had assembled them into a paperback called

Hemingway: The Wild Years, about which Mary was furious, but there was no way to prevent it. I read this collection of newspaper articles Hemingway had written in Toronto and in Europe as a correspondent. They were extremely good— nothing to be furious about—and I decided that we would publish his collected journalism under the title *Byline: Ernest Hemingway*. It was a success and is still in print. A second collection appeared as *Dateline Toronto*, consisting of all his columns in the *Toronto Star* and an introduction by me.

In the end, I introduced most of his posthumous works— not that my purpose was to steal the limelight, but that I knew what editing needed to be done, to begin with, and then explained in a preface. It was easier to do it myself than to ask some busy novelist or critic to do the job. When I made one or two overtures I got no enthusiastic response.

The next posthumous work was *Islands in the Stream*, originally planned in three parts. One was set in Bimini and featured fictionalized versions of his sons; another dealt with a U-boat chase in which his autobiographical hero tried to sink a German sub (he was lucky to get out of that alive); and the third part, as I recall, was again about fishing and the boys.

Hemingway had outlined this three-part work as early as my father's lifetime, I think. But it got pulled apart and reassembled in different versions before he got down to writing it. His first idea, which had us all wondering, was that there would be three parts—land, sea, and air—but the sea was the only one that finally saw the light of print.

Since he had called one part "The Island and the Stream," it seemed to me appropriate to make the title *Islands in the Stream*—romance incarnate. Besides, Hemingway liked poetic images for his titles. The laboring oar in publishing *Islands in the Stream* was wielded by Carlos Baker. It is still on my conscience that his role in editing the manuscript was never formally acknowledged.

The Nick Adams Stories were our next venture, a selection of unfinished works. The critics scolded me (and him) because they were not top-flight stories. We were also scolded for *Islands in the Stream*, but somebody whom I had thought rather hostile to Scribners and to me, Edmund Wilson, came to our defense in a wonderful review in *The New Yorker*. He argued that Scribners had a perfect right to do some editing so as to make the work publishable. The essential thing was that readers should know the text was not as Hemingway had left it, and this we had made clear. That was our practice from first to last in the books by Hemingway that we brought out posthumously.

I may add that the reason I was aware of Wilson's fundamental hostility toward us was that he had worked on a book on John Peale Bishop and had clashed with both Perkins and my father. My father said to Perkins, "Really, that man is a son of a bitch." But Perkins, always the urbane gentleman, added, "But an unconscious one." After my father died, I had some dealings with Edmund Wilson that showed how ferocious he could be. He had corrected something in one of Scott Fitzgerald's works, and believed we hadn't put this emendation in the later edition. He wrote a nasty letter. The fact was, we were in the right and he had made a mistake. This effected a wonderful transformation. I suggested in a letter to him that before writing another disagreeable letter, I wished he would make sure of his facts. He replied rather wistfully about his angry letter; he was contrite about having scolded us. And then he vindicated our handling of literary remains in posthumous editing.

We were once Wilson's publisher. In the thirties we brought out *Axel's Castle* and *I Thought of Daisy*. He left us because my father and Max, for a clear and good reason, did not want to publish *The Wound and the Bow*, a most interesting collection of critical essays (1941). The "wound and the bow" refers to the legend of Philoctetes in the play by Sophocles. Philoctetes was a Greek marooned by his companions on an island during the Trojan War. He had a magic bow, which could do great damage, but he also had a very disagreeable-smelling wound, no doubt gangrenous— hence his being put out of the way. But the Greeks were soon told by one of the gods that they couldn't win the war unless they got Philoctetes and his bow back into action against Troy. So Neoptolemus and Odysseus tricked Philoctetes into coming back with his bow by pretending that they were other than themselves. The application to literary criticism is that the artist suffers from a wound, which has affected his life and his relations with other people—he's a loner—but he has a magic bow, the power to produce art.

Applying this notion in his book, Edmund Wilson "explained" Hemingway by positing his great insecurity about his masculinity. Perkins and my father knew that if they published this, Hemingway would be out the door. (In fact, Ernest was so outraged that he wanted to kill Wilson.) The decision was a hard one to make. I have great admiration for Edmund Wilson, who, though he was not a pleasant person, was a great man. So we lost Wilson but kept Hemingway. If we had kept Wilson, we would have had to publish his *Memoirs of Hecate County* (1946), fiction so full of sexuality it landed in the law courts. I can't imagine Scribners in that period publishing those episodes of Wilson's life or imagination. Today, of course, the book could be taught in high school. So we would have lost Wilson one way or the other.

Against my previous judgment I eventually published in 1985 another Hemingway book about bullfighting in Spain, *The Dangerous Summer*. For years after its 1960 serialization in *Life* magazine, I resisted others' urging me to do it. I did not think it was strong enough to stand in hardcover. Finally, I had it edited by a young man named Michael Pietsch, a tyro editor but extremely bright, who did a splendid job. It turned out a very readable book, beautifully introduced by James Michener.

We also had a huge mass of fictional material that we finally carved into the shape of a novel, *The Garden of Eden*, published in 1986. Although there was a wonderful short story in the lot called "The Elephant Hunt" and some marvelous scenes, I saw no way at first to make a book from the fragments. But Michael Pietsch said we ought to try it. We got a young editor named Tom Jenks to work on it and by cutting and condensing he made a very good book. Some people growled but the literary world and many general readers came into possession of Hemingway scenes and characters they would never have met with otherwise. The last thing I instigated was an omnibus volume of short stories published in 1987 that I called The Finca Vigía Edition, after his home in Cuba.

In the mid-1970s, Mary Hemingway wrote her memoirs, *How It Was*, which I was ready to publish. She sent in several chapters, which I edited with the help of some of my colleagues. We edited them heavily, too heavily. We didn't touch her material, but made suggestions in the interest of fluency, organization, liveliness. It was the kind of editing Jacques Barzun has properly decried as "creeping creativity." It was my fault. Mary went through the roof. She "fired" me, saying, "You can publish Hemingway, but you can't publish me." Yet our relations remained good for other publishing purposes.

The Enduring Hemingway was an anthology published in 1974. I prepared it for the Book-of-the-Month Club and then sold it as a Scribners book. In the preface I ventured an idea I believe to be true, which is that Hemingway was influenced by Joyce's *Dubliners*. The Joyce book was part of the Modern Library series that was so close to Hemingway's heart. These are stories—quite short—of epiphanies in the life of people in Dublin. I believe Hemingway got from them the idea of writing about epiphanies in his own boyhood.

Mary Hemingway, who was in Ketchum when I wrote about that possibility, asked me not to publish it; she didn't want Hemingway linked with Joyce. But I held my ground. External facts lent the hypothesis plausibility. Joyce had invented a poignant and poetic short-story form; those tales of Dubliners are masterpieces. Hemingway probably read them, and he did know Joyce in Paris. Some of Hemingway's stories—"The Three-Day Blow," "The End of Something" —betray a Joyce-like art of composition.

One of the indispensable critical guides to Hemingway is Carlos Baker's *The Writer as Artist*. I knew Carlos well personally and liked him enormously. I first met him when I was an undergraduate and he was on the Princeton faculty. I wasn't a student of his, but I was aware of him and of his interest in Hemingway. He also wrote about Robert Frost and had little interest in the school of Allen Tate and John Crowe Ransom as critics.

Baker's devotion to Hemingway's work was manifest. So when Hemingway died, I immediately got in touch with Baker, and, with Mary's permission, asked him to do an authorized biography, assuring him that we would make all the material available.

Baker's idea was to present with the utmost accuracy all the facts. He had no desire to psychoanalyze Hemingway or interpose critical judgments of the works. He would tell what actually happened. The intellectuals in a body jumped all over Baker for writing "in an unimaginative manner"—

they did not understand what he had intended to do and succeeded in doing.

When I give a lecture on Hemingway, people come up to me and raise the point again. I say, "Look, anybody who writes about Hemingway has to go to Baker's book." Why criticize a work for not doing something the author did not want to do? Baker defended himself by saying that ideas were idiots and facts were real. Baker got a raw deal from the New York literary intelligentsia, but their condescension shows how really unperceptive, *uncritical* they were.

I think that Baker, with his modesty, quiet manners, unfailing courtesy, and high moral standards, was sometimes embarrassed by Hemingway, who was repeatedly a two-timer and not above despicable tricks. But that did not lessen Baker's loving admiration of the works. My working relations and friendship with Baker lasted throughout his life. I never did anything on or about Hemingway without consulting Baker.

Together we did the selection and editing of Hemingway's letters. That is another thing for which I'll have to account to Ernest in the hereafter. Hemingway left strict instructions that his letters should not be published. But, with Mary's approval, I published them—and I think I did the right thing. To begin with, he had kidded my father about publishing his letters, so he had thought of such a thing. Second, I believe his letters show a side of him that nothing else in his work does, and it is a very nice side. I considered that I was justified. It is well known that Virgil left instructions for the *Aeneid* to be burned after his death. Fortunately, not all literary executors obey such requests.

Malcolm Cowley also wrote about Hemingway, notably a major biographical article that was published in *Life* in 1949 and helped put Hemingway back on the map at a time when his fortunes were quite low. Subsequently, I had a little unhappiness with Cowley, because he wanted to publish some letters that I blocked. A young man had letters of Ernest Hemingway's and wouldn't let anybody see them unless he could have the right to publish them. I wouldn't fall for that power play. We could stop him from publishing them, and we did, and Cowley was very upset about it, because he saw it as damaging the possibility of a book in which these letters would figure importantly. I think they were letters between Hemingway and Morley Callaghan.

A. E. Hotchner, well known as a friend of Hemingway's, was his unofficial *comprador*, serving, helping, arranging things. Somebody has said he was an ashtray emptier; he was much more than that. For one thing, Hemingway was fond of him. For another, whoever knew Hemingway in that fashion became proprietary about him, and Hotchner, as Hemingway's great pal, aroused enmity by not wanting to share him with anybody else.

Hotchner and I had our adversarial moments. Believing that he had Hemingway in his hip pocket, he resented anybody else having any say in literary matters affecting his idol. On one occasion Hemingway wrote an introduction for a school text that I turned down because it was dreadfully bad. It was jocular, saying that Faulkner was a drunk, among other things—Hemingway at his worst. It took nerve for me to say it should not be published. George Plimpton wanted it for the *Paris Review*, but I blocked that. Whereupon Hotchner came to me and said, "You know, Papa's very upset. You should not interfere in this way." I stood by my guns, and Hemingway never blamed me. (Years after his death, the *Paris Review* finally succeeded in obtaining permission directly from Ernest's estate to publish the piece.)

I had no dealings with Hemingway's children until after his death. Even then I was permitted few contacts because

Mary alone was in charge of the literary estate. I had my territory marked out for me, and if I had ventured out beyond it, it would have ended my professional relationship with Mary. It was not until the end of her life that I got to know the sons and work with them on publishing *The Garden of Eden* and the collected stories. My main contact was with Patrick, a versatile and brilliant man with whom it was a pleasure to meet and work; we hit it off extremely well. His elder brother Jack, an outstanding sportsman and author of a fine book of memoirs, was no less supportive.

Looking back, I am bound to say that working with Hemingway was rather like being strapped in an electric chair. All the electrodes were always in place, and it would need just the flicking of a switch to ruin me. I might do something quite innocently that would be taken amiss and I would be in outer darkness forever. It was hard. It required constant diplomacy to keep everything smooth. I don't think it made me cowardly, but it made me nervous.

On My Own

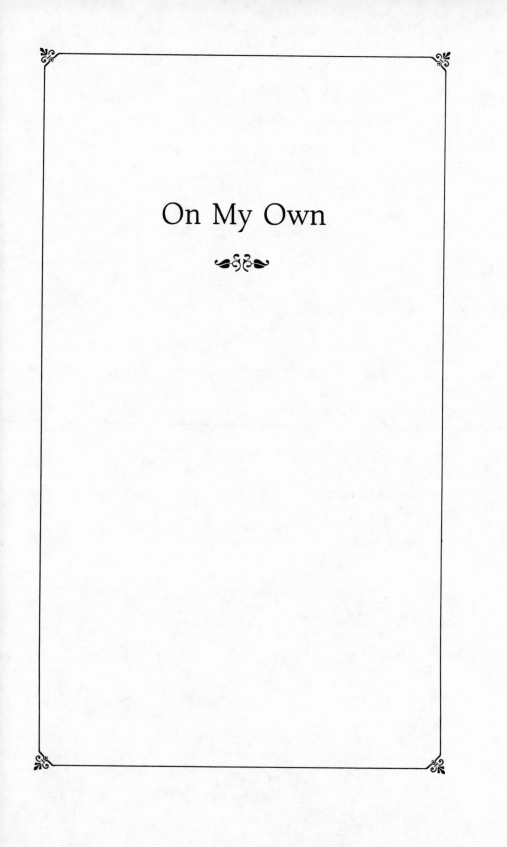

My father's death at the age of sixty-one did not come as a surprise to the family. It was sad and difficult for us, but we knew that his serious heart ailment would carry him off suddenly.

I have mentioned how, in 1952, I began to try running the company, though I had but a wafer-thin education in publishing. The mistakes I made and have indicated were in large part due to my failure to see that I should recruit a top publishing person to run the company with me. The firm suffered as well from what I have called the Perkins cult: if it wasn't literary fiction, it wasn't worth doing, and we spent time fishing for novelistic talent too optimistically. Promise is not enough. We published books in which talent was present but only in the germ. So our fiction went down all too noticeably. Once at a cocktail party a bookseller said to me, "I've learned that we can't trust Scribners' list anymore."

It was a paradoxical situation: at that same time, we had some best-sellers that Brague and Burroughs Mitchell had brought in; and because these books were excellent financially, their success kept us from making changes in policy.

In other words, the company seemed stronger than it was. Its real strength came only when we became more diversified in the books we published.

For a while, everything conspired to delay our reformation. It was easier to publish in those days—the agents were not as powerful as now. The fight for the blockbuster had not set in. The author's demands—or some authors'—were not so coercive as they have become. But gradually publishing became a large-scale money game in which advances and auctions of paperback rights were the chief concern. It required ample financial resources month after month. Not having the means, we were being pushed out of trade publishing. And life was not made easier by our losing money on the many "promising" authors who failed to make the grade for us.

At one point in these doldrums, Robert Giroux called on me and then took my wife and me to the opera. We went on to chat with him at the Opera Club, and he told me that he was interested in a job such as Perkins had had at Scribners. I considered the suggestion but decided it would be hard to put Giroux over the heads of Brague and Mitchell. If I had, it would have been the best possible thing for the company. Giroux is a great man of letters, a great editor, and a great publisher.

In the education and reference book departments, we were also limping, but our recovery will be told on another page. That is where I really did do something original and successful. Looking back, I find it difficult to compute a total from the negative and the positive in my performance. I am bound to be critical of myself, because I was culpably ignorant. Yet I managed to keep Hemingway under the difficulties described earlier; I held on to our other first-rate authors; and I finally got the hang of things and innovated.

*   *   *

But before detailing that phase of my history, I must say a word about an important figure of the transitional period: James Jones. He had been first a Perkins author; Max's editing of Jones's *From Here to Eternity* (1951) was considerable. Hemingway can describe eating a boiled egg and putting salt and pepper on it, and without more words he adds something to the description in a manner that cannot be imitated. Now Jones in his first drafts would give commonplace details that were just—commonplace, mere clutter. Perkins would say, "Don't tell people what they know."

Jones once asked me to lunch and during the meal propounded much pseudoscience about diet. He would take nothing but water for several days, and from the ensuing symptoms would deduce great benefit for his health. This quack medicine rather depressed me. In the same vein, he went on to talk about his desire to learn mathematics and science in a serious way. As he talked, he downed four or five martinis, which did not seem to augur well for his applying himself to these difficult fields. But at his request I did suggest some books with which to make a start.

The truth is, his intellectual ambitions were pathetic. Here was a young man who had a real gift and didn't know exactly what it was for and how best to develop it. He was the toast of literary New York for a while and did not adjust to this new role. He bragged incredibly about his sexual prowess with call girls and others, like a very young boy—and distastefully. I did not take to that style of confidence from an author, for there is nothing to say in return—ohs and ahs are soon exhausted.

After Perkins, Jones produced *Some Came Running*, and better still, *The Thin Red Line*. That was encouraging; it was full of good things, and Jones could create characters as well as tell an interesting story. I never got around to reading the novella called *The Pistol*, but by that time his fiction was turning slovenly and scatological with little else to sustain interest.

On *Go to the Widow Maker* he finally asked for a bigger advance than we could afford, and although some of the Scribners editors thought that James Jones was God's gift to modern literature, I was glad to have him leave us. My colleagues were utterly dismayed.

I do not regret my decision. He can hardly be said to have written a good book after *The Thin Red Line* (1962). And his behavior had turned deliberately bizarre. He came to the office wearing dark-colored motorcycle goggles that covered half his face, spoke outrageous French, and boasted of taking a pulpit from a French church and turning it into a bar. Whether it was meant to be provocative or served some private need of self-bolstering, I did not feel I was called on to play along.

Hemingway couldn't stand Jones. He may have been jealous of the success of *From Here to Eternity*. What he said to Perkins and my father was "It's the end of writing," and then, "Of course, you're doing well with your Corporal Jones" (the worst insult that he could think of). "I mean you've hitched your wagon to the shit wagon." It was childish, no doubt. Hemingway was never very generous toward other Scribners authors. He would refer darkly to Thomas Wolfe's "chickenshit estate"—one sourpuss remark after another.

From Here to Eternity was the first big movie sale and the New American Library paid the then huge price of $100,000 for the reprint rights; it would be $10 million today. For the time being, it put us on the map as a very strong trade house. With *Not as a Stranger* and *The Last Angry Man*, we had more blockbusters than anyone else.

But it was a self-destroying form of success. Once a Scribners author turned into a best-seller, the agents and other publishers tried to get him or her away by offers of advances we could not afford. Morton Thompson, the author of *Not as a Stranger*, was a self-taught man, extremely neurotic, extremely vain. He was so tense that if you said something that disturbed him, you saw the sweat come out on his forehead. When he was writing his novel, he referred to the *tragos* of the Greeks. To him, *tragos* and *tragic* were parallel with *ethos* and *ethic*. Well, Greek is not to be guessed from what happens in English. I said, "Mr. Thompson, that's not quite right. I've studied Greek. In ancient Greek, *tragos* means goat or armpit odor." He said, "That's not true. I read it in Quiller-Couch." I'm sure he didn't, though Quiller-Couch may have derived the word *tragedy* from "goat-song" in Greek. Thompson also thought that since there was *hysteria*, so there should be, again by analogy, *hysteros*. I had to say, "No, you are confusing different roots." He replied, "You're wrong," and his book came out with both of those blunders. He was immune to correction.

I asked him if he could give us a contract on his next book. His answer was "No. If you had a contract from me, that would be like your having a whip in your safe that you could take out and use on me whenever you wanted to." So we didn't get the contract. Some four or five weeks later he died and almost immediately after that his wife committed suicide. His brother-in-law, Sylvester Pindyke, then inherited one of the great best-selling "properties."

It was discovered that a few passages in *Not as a Stranger* had been taken verbatim from the memoirs of a doctor. There ensued a plagiarism complaint. Two or three of these passages dealt with the staunchness of a Christian Scientist as a patient, and another with a doctor who was paid in chickens instead of money.

What plagiarism Thompson had committed was trivial; he was not a plagiarist in the true sense of the word. He doubtless had made notes of these facts to use later as lively bits of verisimilitude and probably forgot that he'd taken them from someone else. But the widow of the doctor who was the author of the details was a trained nurse, and she raised an enormous fuss. Since we had a movie contract under way, we had to settle pretty quickly at gunpoint.

We also had a big suit about *From Here to Eternity*. A man who had been with Jones in the army was called Maggio, and one of the characters in the novel was called Maggio. The case was handled by Horace Manges, who was an astute advocate for authors and publishers in the legal arena—or lions' den. He argued that a writer of fiction must rely on his experience and that of the people he has known. In the absence of libel or any other tort, he has a right to what he has learned. It was an accident that the name Maggio had been used. Evidence turned up that after Jones's book had become famous, Maggio made a deal with a magazine to sell his own story. That punctured his balloon, and the judge confirmed our contention that writers of fiction necessarily take life as their material source of ideas. The decision became a precedent for other cases.

Sad to say, with every best-seller you are almost sure to have a lawsuit. Scribners and Jones even had a second. We were taken to court for obscenity. The now familiar argument was made: a book must be taken as a whole, not one passage at a time, and must be judged by contemporary standards. Horace Manges read the entire book to the jury over several days. They had to swallow every single word. At one point occurred the phrase "in a pig's ass" or something of the kind, and one juror asked, "What did you say?" My good friend and golf partner Horace, who was the most dignified of men, repeated it, with exquisite enunciation.

*　　　*　　　*

Alan Paton, another of our highly successful writers, had first been read by Perkins, not long before Perkins's death, and we published *Cry, the Beloved Country* in 1948, to the author's satisfaction and ours. But again there was a disagreeable sequel. Jonathan Cape, the English publisher, was in New York, and Perkins told Cape what a wonderful book he had just signed up. Cape should publish it in England. "In fact," he added, "it would have been more logical for you to bring it out first in England, because it's about the once-English colony of South Africa."

Cape published the English edition. Then, when Paton finished his next, *Too Late the Phalarope* (1953), Cape tried to take the book away from us. He managed to get the Canadian rights and then went after the foreign rights. I vowed I would never speak to him again. It was the first time (and the last) that I resolved to snub a fellow publisher and carried out my vow. Since then his type of sharp practice has become common form.

I wrote to Hemingway about the incident because Cape was Hemingway's publisher abroad. I couched it in understatement: "Cape," I wrote, "certainly has a gift for the unexpected." Hemingway, who did not like Cape, wanted to know more, but in the end kept him as a publisher; it would have been awkward to take all his books elsewhere.

What was disappointing was that Paton himself never stood up for us. We had made his fame and fortune in this country, but more than once he let Cape take advantage of us. In the struggle that seems endemic in author-publisher relations, fairness, gratitude, and loyalty are not virtues that belong to either side as a class. They are strictly individual traits.

Paton gave us one more excellent book, which he called *Debbie, Go Home*—a collection of very fine short stories of

South Africa. I retitled the book *Tales from a Troubled Land*. Thereafter, his output fell off. He did a book on Jan Hendrik Hofmeyr as a notable political figure in the government of South Africa. It was extremely dull, but I published it (without irony) as *South African Tragedy*. Then he did a really bad book on Archbishop Clayton. Still I published it, one more act of devotion beyond the call of duty for us.

Paton's ultimate display of indifference occurred when he submitted his final novel, *Ah, But Your Land Is Beautiful* in 1981. Oxford tried to get it ahead of us, and all Paton said was "You and Oxford must fight it out." We had been faithfully publishing his obvious losers, which Oxford was religiously turning down one after the other. Meanwhile, Paton professed great friendship for me and got friendship in return. I remonstrated mildly about the Oxford incident, but made no change in my response to his amiabilities. (We succeeded, I might add, in defending our American turf from our British brethren.)

Paton was a superb writer and I kept urging him to produce more fiction. His nonfiction was mechanical and dry and his two-volume autobiography was prosaic. Yet we published it as he saw fit, for his life had been one of exemplary courage and integrity. As a person he was likable and not without humor. His ordinary conversation was always full of remarks meant to sting a little, though not necessarily his interlocutor. This critical tone went well with the bark in his speaking voice. He thought of himself as I thought of him—as a genius.

Of Gerald Green's three books under our imprint the first was *The Last Angry Man*. It was about the author's father, a Jewish doctor in Brooklyn. The story had a poignancy and perceptiveness that caught the public. My mother called me up when she had read up to the point where the doctor has a heart attack and said, "If anything happens to that doctor, I'll never speak to you again."

Gerald Green's second novel lacked the force and the substance of the first. This often happens. First novels come out of people's lives and the lore of their families and friends. The next are likely to have the consistency of ectoplasm. The third and last was *The Lotus Eaters*. It contained some sexy scenes by a swimming pool, which made some of my friends think that Scribners had come of age at last. It is true that the firm had always hung back from publishing things that were ahead of the mores. This hesitancy, which was certainly not advantageous financially, probably had to do with the fact that our family name was on each book. The act of publishing—making public—thereby became more personal than if we had been called, say, "Random House." Scribners is a signature, and the bearer of the name is implicated with the contents of the message.

Of course, my father was a regular Victorian, and I began in the same frame of mind; yet he published Hemingway and Fitzgerald, who for their time were "advanced," "outspoken," "uninhibited," though now they would no longer deserve these epithets.

At the time my father died, Lindbergh's *The Spirit of St. Louis* (1953) was a work-in-progress, so the responsibility for it when finished fell on my fledgling shoulders. Lindbergh could be very difficult. Once, lunching with him at the Racquet Club, I ventured to argue with him. As we exchanged views, he was looking at me with steely blue eyes, and suddenly I said to myself, "You're talking to a man who flew a single-engine plane alone across the Atlantic Ocean! How brash and stupid to bandy words!" I hoisted the white flag immediately, knowing the man had a will like Caesar's.

I should add that the Racquet Club was all agog at having Charles Lindbergh there.

He was the most fussy of authors, living or dead. He would measure the difference between a semicolon and a colon to make sure each was what it ought to be. To him, every detail in the book had as much significance as if it were a moving part in his airplane. The book was a Book-of-the-Month Club selection, and I was shown the first copy. I riffled through and saw that the type had been pied on two pages. It was sheer gobbledygook, the lines upside down, backwards, or out of order. I nearly fainted at the sight itself, and again at the thought that it would be my cheerful duty to tell Lindbergh. I wasn't going to conceal it.

I called up and said: "An awful thing has happened to your book. A couple of pages have been badly pied by the typesetter. We can fix it in subsequent printings, but we can't fix it now. It's out at the Book-of-the-Month Club." Praise God, he said to me: "Oh, don't worry about that. That'll just make the first printing more valuable." He had brushed the catastrophe aside. Ever after that, I felt a deep gratitude to him.

Lindbergh being a friend of Bill Jovanovich, and the latter being now publisher at Harcourt Brace, our Charles would leave us when it came to his next book. He had in fact given me part of a manuscript. He was in the Philippines at the time, where I wrote to him saying, "I'm sorry you're leaving us. I'm returning the manuscript you left with us, and I hope you will have great success with it." I was not remonstrating, but he apparently didn't like to have anybody do the gallant thing. He wrote me a twenty-page letter explaining why he was doing what he was doing. I think my natural gesture had heaped coals of fire on his head, as St. Paul puts it, because I had taken it quite gracefully and without a scintilla of rebuke.

One more tale of early days. Our editorial meetings were held around a table, each editor suggesting and criticizing freely. As I think of those discussions now, I am bound to admit that publishers are hapless victims to the know-it-all attitude—myself not the least opinionated. At one meeting, Elinor Parker mentioned a book on crewel embroidery by one Erica Wilson. We didn't know anything about it or her. We had never done a book on embroidery, and it seemed a remote domain.

I said, "Do you really think you would sell any of those?"

She replied, "Yes. Erica Wilson gives a course on needlework and canvas work in New York. Her students would buy it. There's a good deal of general interest, and an advertisement for the course appeared in *The New Yorker*."

Grudgingly, I said, "Go ahead, then."

We produced a gorgeous book with full-color plates from Princeton Polychrome and the book was a smash hit. We sold that very expensive book in the tens of thousands, and it kept on selling indefinitely. What is more, it generated a whole line of books in the field, as well as in beadwork and other crafts. Produced with an eye to artistic presentation, all of them became a major part of our publishing output. When other publishers clambered aboard this bandwagon, it amounted to a literary revolution in this particular range of hobbies.

The experience also taught us a lesson. It showed that publishing was not a trade limited to novels and biographies. The idea of publishing—especially of our publishing—had to be broadened to take in all other subjects of public interest. We were at last weaned away from our exclusive devotion to fiction. Weren't we terribly smart to get into this world of needlework? No! We had to be dragged into it. We were only smart enough to see success when it came and hit us in the eye.

Publishers
and Publishing

❧❦❧

Toward the end of World War II, the reprint house of Grosset & Dunlap was put up for sale by its family owners. A number of people bid for it, and a group of publishers bought it jointly. The group included Harry Scherman of the Book-of-the-Month Club; Arthur Thornhill of Little, Brown; Bennett Cerf of Random House; Cass Canfield of Harper's; the Curtis Publishing Company, which published the *Saturday Evening Post*; and my father. Grosset & Dunlap reissued fiction in cheap editions, as well as children's books. The purchasers thought it desirable to keep it in existence. I succeeded my father on the board and the chairmanship rotated among the new owners. In the course of time, Grosset & Dunlap created Bantam Books as a paperback imprint, which brought us all into that busy world of the "mass market" in a more immediate way.

I had mixed emotions about the move. I was not keen about paperback books as they were then, and I could not see what special advantage there was for us in the investment that we might not have had from investing in any other company. But I derived an indirect benefit. The first president of Bantam Books was Walter Pitkin, who was soon succeeded by an amazingly brilliant man, Oscar Dystel, who had worked for a little magazine called *Coronet*. He was a spectacularly effective person in paperback publishing and built Bantam Books into one of the strongest houses of its kind in the country. He and I became very good friends and I learned a lot from him during our friendship of many years.

Though in principle none of the owners of Grosset & Dunlap should have profited more than the rest, I think Random House did, from overseeing the publishing of low-priced children's books and receiving compensation for the service. For my part, I felt rather that I was part-owner of a competing publishing house. Even so, I contributed one business idea to the combine. The firm had difficulty in getting its share of paperback Westerns and other popular genres and decided to offer authors higher royalties, covering the cost by raising the price on these books from twenty-five to thirty cents. My contribution was to suggest that if the price could be raised on one class of books, why not raise it across the board? My plea for logic resulted in increasing the price of paperback books.

On other points I proved wrong—for instance, when Grosset & Dunlap wanted to turn The Hardy Boys series into paperbacks. In my conservative spirit, I thought it a poor idea, believing that the youngsters would miss the feel and appearance of the old edition. Grosset & Dunlap went ahead and was proved right.

Some awkward situations arose. When Scribners had a strong best-seller, Bantam thought it should have the inside track in the form of a first refusal on the paperback. For us that would have been counterproductive: we might get a better offer from one of the other paperback houses. In consequence, I was thought a traitor when I denied Bantam its *droit du seigneur* and sold *Not as a Stranger* or *From Here to Eternity* to competing firms. Victor Weybright took *From Here to Eternity* for the New American Library—a characteristic coup. He was a flamboyant, imaginative publisher who went for the biggest books and made the biggest offers.

Other disagreements with Grosset & Dunlap occurred over children's books. Scribners had a series about Franklin, Jefferson, and other historic Americans, and we thought Grosset virtually copied the series. I began to think that the joint venture yielded nothing for Scribners or any of the other participants. Finally, there came a break. Grosset & Dunlap produced overseas and without our authority an edition of *Peter Pan* in their popular children's series. The book was done up in atrocious taste, as if aimed at the dime-store market. At that time, Scribners still had the U.S. copyright on *Peter Pan*. It was naturally quite valuable, and Mary Martin was starring in the play on Broadway, which boosted book sales. Because the new edition was printed abroad, it would jeopardize copyright if imported into the United States. That in turn would have been a catastrophe for the Hospital for Sick Children in England, which owned the original copyright and counted on American royalties.

So I had the unpleasant task of telling the people at Grosset that they couldn't sell their edition, of which they had an enormous number of copies in stock, in the United States. They could sell them only in Canada.

I was pounced on mercilessly: "Charlie, why can't you be a team player?" But that was not the right question. I had a fiduciary responsibility for the copyright, and I remained adamant. John O'Connor, Grosset's peppery partisan, accused me of disloyalty. That really angered me. They had been careless and had jeopardized the copyright in the first place, and now unless I was a "good sport" about it I would be guilty of misdoing.

At the same time, I did sympathize. I wished there were some way I could rescue them from their predicament. But I couldn't see any and our lawyer didn't see any. They then tried to prove that our copyright was shaky, which was hardly an endearing act from colleagues preaching loyalty.

That step galvanized me into a rather impetuous decision on my part to get out of Grosset & Dunlap. To withdraw was no doubt right for Scribners, but I rashly said that I would be satisfied simply to get back what my father had paid for his share of the company—some two decades earlier—as I wanted to sever the relationship in a generous spirit. Later, the remaining partners decided to sell the whole company on the open market, and it was sold for a huge sum in which we no longer shared. My decision had cost me dearly. I was young, and I had to pay the price for the lessons I needed. I learned to hold my fire and investigate more thoroughly before making a move.

In his interview for the oral history archive at Columbia University, Cerf called me foolish for leaving Grosset & Dunlap. There's no question about it, but then he added, "We tried to talk him out of it," and that is not so. They tried nothing of the sort. On the contrary, they were over-joyed at the unexpected increase of their stock. They did not match my foolishness by trying to dissuade me.

In that phase of my publishing career, as I said, I did not like paperbacks; and as recorded earlier, I reclaimed the original licenses of our best backlist books so as to reissue them in hardcover. But in the upshot I did not do it, because paperbacks, in a new, better designed, and more expensive style, swept over the nation. I followed suit. Everybody thought I was preternaturally clever to have taken back the licenses so I could publish the books in paperback myself. I was given credit for the opposite of what I intended. Such is the way motives are interpreted.

The Scribners paperback series started out as student editions, primarily for college use. Sold at a short discount, they were aimed at the institutions, not the general public. But the college bookstores complained, because they wanted to get the profit of the full discount—forty percent instead of twenty percent.

We complied and brought out the books as a series called The Scribner Library with a cover specially designed in a grayish, grasslike pattern. The collection became one of the most successful of the new "quality paperback" lines in the country. Quality paperbacks sold at a higher price because they were not the usual small pocket books, but full-sized with good margins and good print. Their success justified my effort to get back the rights to important Scribners authors.

Early on, I wrote an ad for The Scribner Library that said in part, "It isn't how many books we have on the list, but how important and salable they are." This was printed in red and black ink on a two-page spread in *Publishers Weekly*. To my surprise, *PW* wrote an editorial about the ad, agreeing that it wasn't how many paperbacks you published that mattered, but the quality and the demand for them. A further result was that *The New York Times* discontinued its best-seller listing of trade paperbacks. Since some eighty to ninety percent were Scribner books, there was no point in running it.

It was as a Grosset & Dunlap partner that I first came to know Cass Canfield; after a while, it was as a golfing partner. We used to play with Horace Manges and Ray Harwood, the head of Harper's, whom I also saw when we were both trustees of Princeton University Press. We were close friends, and a very pleasant relationship it was. I had a family feeling about both of them, too, because they had also been friends of my father's. Ray Harwood was a very good businessman. Cass was an editing and publishing president at Harper's, while Ray dealt with the business side—a common pairing in publishing firms. Fortunately for our golf games, which we usually played on or around Columbus Day, none of us was good enough to be the best: we were equally bad. But Cass, Harwood, and Manges had had more practice: they were much older than I was.

It seems to me, looking back, that it's a miracle that I survived our golf games, we suffered so many mishaps. Once on a very precipitous hill, with a deep ditch at the end, one of our golf carts was allowed to roll free. I ran after it, as if after a horse, jumped into it, and managed to stop it just before it went over the edge.

On another occasion a twosome somehow jammed their golf cart into the railing along a footpath and couldn't get it out. I climbed over to the other side to push the cart back and get it going up the hill. Suddenly the thought struck me that I was wrestling a heavy vehicle that would most likely fall back on me and drown me in the mud. My companions remained benignly oblivious of the fact that my life had been at risk.

Yet another time, one of our quartet stepped back from the tee into a pond. I jumped into what looked like water but was mud, to a depth I found alarming. But I finally got footing enough to get my arms under my friend and pull him out. He went home, but I kept on playing, and, to my astonishment, hit the ball better than I had ever done in my life. The catastrophe would have excused me from playing bad golf, so I never played better.

A few days after this adventure I had a call from my companion in the mud: "Do you know what happened to my driver? It wasn't in my bag." I said, "I will tell you, as only Sherlock Holmes could do. I know exactly where your driver is. It's at the bottom of the pond behind the tee at the tenth hole. They tried to fish it out, but it's still stuck there."

Among my other colleagues at Grosset & Dunlap, I liked best Donald Klopfer and Bennett Cerf. As everybody knows, Bennett was something of an *enfant terrible*, but he was a first-rate publisher, and so was Klopfer. I always enjoyed meeting Klopfer, because of his rather courtly manners and pleasant conversation. Bennett could also say pleasant things, notably about some of Scribners' books, which was very gracious of him.

With Arthur Thornhill I had dealings not only through Grosset & Dunlap but also in American Book Publishers Council affairs as well. Alfred McIntyre, his predecessor at Little, Brown, had been a great friend of both Whitney Darrow's and my father's. He was a legendary figure, a sensible, friendly man of the old school of publishing. Ordinarily, publishers are polite and companionable with one another. It's an agreeable fraternity, and puts me in mind of the motto carved on the wall above a fireplace at Eton: "Strive mightily, but eat and drink as friends." In my day, the publishing fraternity in New York certainly strove mightily—from time to time stealing authors from other publishers; that was considered fair game—but they would not cease to eat and drink as friends.

At the age of fifteen, in the nineteenth century, the first Nelson Doubleday came to work for Scribners as a stockboy. He worked himself up through various ranks in the company until he became manager of *Scribner's Magazine*. From his book about his experience in publishing, I gather that he left Scribners because my grandfather was too cantankerous. He would go to my grandfather and say, "Don't you think this is a good idea for a book—or for a magazine article?" My grandfather would cheerfully reply that it was a terrible idea. That happened once too often, and Nelson Doubleday *primus* went off and established his own firm. I'm sure that a fair sprinkling of our authors followed him there.

In my own era, Doubleday once sent me a manuscript with a good deal of Hemingway material quoted in it and asked me to see if the amount was within the bounds of "fair use." As I was going to St. Bartholomew's Church and the Doubleday office was nearby, I thought I would return the galleys to the editor who was working on it, Kate Medina. (She herself later became a famous figure in publishing.) At Doubleday, on Park Avenue, I said I had something to deliver and was told by the receptionist that the service entrance was around the corner.

For a minute, I wondered whether my coat was that shabby, but I meant to have my way—and finally succeeding in delivering the manuscript. Weeks later I sat next to Nelson Doubleday III at the Racquet Club, and I told him of my Doubleday adventure. It was a story he could dine out on, I thought—but he was not amused.

I doubt whether Nelson was ever really enamored of publishing. He did not concern himself with the literary side of the business; it was his brother-in-law John Sargent who did that. John Sargent was chief executive at Doubleday for years, and I got to know him very well. Very intelligent, very amusing, and a very good publisher, he was determined that the publishing business should lose none of its prerogatives. He was a good politician for the publishing industry, as I can testify from serving with him on many committees of the American Book Publishers Council.

One of Doubleday's bright young men, Jason Epstein, was the one who thought up the "quality paperback." As I was not given to licensing out copyrights, he got the impression—or took the attitude toward me—that I was an unreconstructed fogy. He brought out a series of children's classics called The Looking Glass Library, many of which had originally been published by Scribners. He advertised these books as being unavailable elsewhere and boasted that he had brought them back into print. I had to remonstrate because most of them were still in print and available from Scribners. Alas, they were also by this time in the public domain and "fair game" for competitors.

A happily different sort of publishing relation developed between me and Bill Jovanovich. He was a friendly contemporary, we lunched together, and we sorted out amicably a few minor contretemps about permission to use or reprint copyrighted material. When I turned down his requests, both sides adhered to their high standard of good manners. Bill, I knew, was brilliant and strong-willed, but few could have had an inkling that he would become the great publishing tycoon of his generation. His turning Harcourt Brace into one of the biggest houses in the world was a great spectacle. For Bill was also a man of letters, an essayist and novelist. He submitted to us one of his books, which I found full of good things and extremely well written; I had the unwelcome task of declining it, which he took with very good grace.

Many of my father's generation of publishers had a paternal attitude toward me. The industry—as it was not yet called— was a small community, in which everybody knew everybody else. By the time the next generation had taken over, I was in closer touch with my father's, who had accepted me as a colleague because of my special status as the heir of the firm. In reality, I was astride the generations, but I leaned to the older side. Scribners never thought of going public. As a result we could not play a stellar role in the auctions for books; we did not have money on the needed scale. By that measure, we were low in the ranking, and it was a severe handicap. On the other hand, since we couldn't simply buy what we wanted, we had to use our wits to get the books we liked to publish and sell them successfully.

We thought up original ideas about creating and marketing books other than fiction, such as reference books—of which more details later. I did not believe that the blockbuster held any promise for a medium-sized company. Some thought me wrong, but nothing that's happened since has led me to revise my judgment. I listened to all the gossip that filled the New York–Boston corridor, but I paid it little more than an amused attention. Perhaps I was not fanatical enough to be the perfect publisher; I simply could not make publishing my whole life. I think—and hope—that I never failed to play my part in the profession. I joined in battles to support freedom of the press. On professional committees and otherwise I met my responsibilities. But I also pursued my intellectual concerns, notably in the history of science; I read new books and not manuscripts only; and I kept up with contemporary ideas.

Among such ideas, those relating to sex in literature found me resistant, not to say prudish. I marveled at Barney Rosset's daring in publishing at the Grove Press the works of Henry Miller and others—the cream of pornography, so to speak. They all seem almost tame in retrospect. But I stood out strongly against censorship; a publisher had the right to publish or not publish whatever he chose. And that meant also that I declined to be bullied by public opinion into publishing something I did not relish.

Nat Wartels, who had smash best-sellers like Dr. Comfort's *Joy of Sex*, kept telling me, in the nicest spirit, that I had far more advantages than I was aware of in my birthright as the inheritor of a famous company. He would say, "The Scribner name wields more power than you realize. You should take advantage of it." He felt that I did not make capital out of the firm's reputation to lure these venturesome new writers. My feeling was the opposite, that we were at a disadvantage in being an old company and so well known; age made young authors think we were old stuffed shirts. Our innovations had to lie in other fields.

The attitude of textbook publishers toward literature differs from that of trade publishers. Theirs is much less of a profession. In the years that I was active in the American Book Publishers Council, I found it hard to reach a meeting of minds with them. They saw theirs as a great business and ours as a literary tea party. Eventually a *modus vivendi* was achieved, thanks to such strong houses as McGraw-Hill, which had both trade and textbook departments. They made possible what was later called the Association of American Publishers.

What was involved in mutual understanding was reprint rights. The textbook publishers were getting the most valuable properties for something like a conventional tip. I took the plunge and drastically increased our permissions charges. Instead of giving the rights to Hemingway's "Snows of Kilimanjaro," one of the greatest stories of all time, for the usual $250, I put it on a royalty basis. I also limited the number of stories by one author that could be used in an anthology. To take more than one was unfair to the author; equally so to skim the cream off the top of the bottle. I regulated that, too.

And I was right. Textbook companies had been coming to the gold mine with a wheelbarrow and helping themselves. They were getting something for little or nothing, and I put a stop to it in the teeth of much resentment. Nor was it a scalping operation. I did not ask for exorbitant sums; it was usually a matter of pennies per copy sold. When I had a chance to talk to the publishers and explain the position, they took the changed order with good grace. The industry followed my lead. More and more publishers charged royalties instead of a flat fee. Having so many authors of the kind in demand for such reprinting, Scribners perhaps benefited more than most others.

In the belief that commercial publishers like Scribners were unable or ill-equipped to handle certain books of scholarly or literary merit, and that university presses could provide that outlet, my grandfather gave Princeton a building, an entire printing plant, and an endowment for what became the Princeton University Press. Today, the several dozens of university presses play an extremely important role in publishing.

The first director of the Princeton University Press was Whitney Darrow, the same Whitney who later became, as I have recounted, business manager at Scribners. In early press days, differentiation between academic and trade publishing was not so clear as it later became. When Yale University wanted to publish a Bicentennial Series, it came to Scribners and we took it on. We did not hesitate to publish works of sociology, science, anthropology, or any other scholarly disciplines. It was only those addressed to small specialist circles that my grandfather could not afford to bring out but thought universities ought to publish.

As the university presses grew stronger, books that used to belong on trade lists, including many works of science, began to drop away—to be picked up by the new species of publishers. By virtue of my personal and family attachment to Princeton, I began to serve on the board of the University Press shortly before 1950. Though I was only twenty-eight years old, I took it as a responsibility that my father had assumed before me and that I could not avoid. Except for a brief break when I was in the navy, I attended the meetings

"Dew Hollow," my family's home in Far Hills, New Jersey.

With my sister, Julia—hardly dressed for a walk in the woods—circa 1925.

My grandfather, Charles Scribner II.

My grandmother, Louise Flagg Scribner.

The Scribner Building, home of the Princeton University Press, designed by Uncle Ernest Flagg.

The Scribner Building, at 597 Fifth Avenue, New York City, also designed by Ernest Flagg.

The Scribner Book Store, looking out toward Fifth Avenue.

My father in his office, circa 1936; his relaxed expression reflected his assumption that my photograph, taken only with available light from the window, would not develop.

Scribners' most famous novelist—and fisherman—Ernest Hemingway, with his bemused editor Max Perkins, in Key West, 1935.

With my mother, Vera Bloodgood Scribner, Master of the Essex Foxhounds (mid 1940s)—here accompanied by her seldom-equestrian son.

The one Scribner the navy sent to sea: the S.S. Charles Scribner being launched by my parents in November 1943.

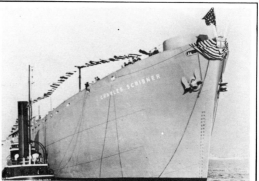

The happiest moment on film: with my bride, Joan, at our wedding on July 16, 1949, in Morristown, New Jersey. Flanking us, with glasses raised, are Joan's parents, Mr. and Mrs. Edwin S. S. Sunderland

With Joan, our son Charlie, and our new daughter-in-law, Ritchie Markoe Scribner, at their Far Hills wedding, August 1979.

Our three sons, from left to right: Blair, Charlie, and John.

With Mary Hemingway at Scribners, April 1970, announcing the posthumous publication of Islands in the Stream.

With Joan and P. D. James in London.

On the ice, Joan entertained authors and other company alike—solo!

regularly, and I got to know almost all the senior members of the faculty, who were either board members, advisers, or authors. It was a wonderful experience to sit next to Harold Dodds, the president, or Dean Root, the head of the faculty, or Henry D. Smyth, one of the architects of the atomic bomb.

After my father left the board, Whitney Darrow became president. He was followed in 1951 by Henry Laughlin, the head of Houghton Mifflin, and then when Laughlin wanted to be less active, I succeeded him six years later. I was president for eleven years, from 1957 to 1968, and missed hardly a meeting. In the beginning, the trustees actively discussed the books to be published. Later, the editorial staff did some of the winnowing, but all the eligible books were presented to the whole board at every meeting.

The Princeton University Press was by design legally and financially independent of the university, but my grandfather made his founding gift with the understanding that the university could at will take over the press lock, stock, and barrel. To be sure, an essential link between the two institutions was implicit in the role faculty members played on the editorial board and the roster of trustees, which included the university president.

In the hundreds of meetings I attended, I heard more scholarly discussions of book projects than I had dreamed of when I agreed to serve. These stood me in good stead when I came to publish Scribners reference books. I had learned how academics think, what they value, what they are willing or not willing to do. Of course, on several occasions at the press, I saw books I would have loved to see Scribners publish, but it never occurred to me to suborn the author in any way.

I have indicated how little Whitney Darrow was interested in books. Their presence was to him the necessary price to pay for the pleasure of running the press as a business concern. That attitude distressed my grandfather, whose primary interest was the books. My father, too, saw the whole purpose of the press as service to scholarship. All they wanted to be sure of was that the management of the press exercised enough business acumen to survive.

In that regard, the press had its ups and downs. It was rather a small satellite in the Princeton galaxy until Datus Smith became the director after World War II. Datus was an absolute whirlwind. It was he who saw to it that the press published Henry Smyth's *Atomic Energy for Military Purposes*. Datus insisted on the highest quality in the books he published, and by his faith and vigor and love of books—to say nothing of his intelligence—he made the press into one of the best in the country. It became and has remained a powerful agent of scholarship.

The momentum was maintained by Datus Smith's successor, Herbert Bailey. Herb first worked as science editor for the press. Soon, all his qualities of mind, coupled with his energy, singled him out as the ideal person to lead the press. Under him, the Princeton University Press greatly helped American scholarship to gain international recognition. A large percentage of its books were sold overseas, far more than the usual proportion of a trade publisher's list.

A Princeton graduate in the Class of 1942, Herb Bailey was just my age. He had studied electrical engineering and literature, a rare combination. These joint interests, literary and scientific, favored our becoming close friends—a good thing for the president and the director of an institution.

One of his innovations was to establish the printing operration as a separate entity. He built the Laughlin Building, a big plant for offset printing, and lodged there all the machinery required for a nearly complete manufacturing business. Now, when one enters the hall of the original press building (the "Scribner Building"), one sees the handsome hall with cantilevered ceilings, built by Ernest Flagg, that originally housed the printing presses and binding machines. Additional buildings and wings have added to the editorial space, and the separate plant has enabled the press to greatly increase its list, with no drop in quality in scholarly substance or book manufacture. With the help of the great book designer P. J. Conkwright, the Princeton University Press has taken its place among the leaders in beautiful bookmaking and continues to garner more than a proportional share of annual design awards.

Bailey also developed a working relationship with Paul Mellon and took over Mellon's Bollingen Books program. The name Bollingen comes from a village in Switzerland where Carl Jung had his country retreat. Through the Bollingen Foundation, Mellon published classics like the *I Ching*, a work of Chinese philosophy; the collected writings of Jung; and a great series on the fine arts. By businesslike methods, Herb Bailey staunched what had been a reckless outflow of funds and made the series more than self-supporting.

Now the press is publishing the Einstein Papers, a monumental project that will continue well into the next century. It was Bob Goheen, then president of the university, who told me that when he went on a trip around the world, the two things that people knew about Princeton were the books of the Princeton University Press and Albert Einstein. And, as Bob added wistfully, neither really belonged to the university.

Ray Harwood of Harper's, my friend, colleague, and fellow trustee, succeeded me in December 1968. Ray was a great president to hold the press together, though he was not a Princeton alumnus. All his life was spent in publishing, and he knew how a publishing company should be run. Of course, Herb Bailey was running it then without any need for help, but Ray was there to lend a hand any time to back him up.

Harold McGraw of McGraw-Hill, a staunch Princetonian, was a couple of years ahead of me in college, and it was he who succeeded Harwood as president of the press in 1972. Harold was then head of one of the most successful and powerful publishing companies in the world. I admired him greatly, not least because in spite of his great position he never got top-lofty. He would come down to the meetings of the press not having had any lunch and would buy packets of peanut butter sandwiches from a cash vending machine just to munch on something before going into the meeting. Always very hard working, he was a decent and thoughtful man, concerned about all aspects of the publishing industry.

Arthur Thornhill joined the board of the press both because he was a Princetonian and because of his publishing experience at Little, Brown. We always wanted to have publishers on the board, and we continue to do so. The editorial board is made up of scholars; the board of trustees attends to the business side and the printing.

The status of the university presses in the life of the country today is what my grandfather envisioned for them in the beginning. Their *raison d'être* is to enable scholarship to be disseminated. But every now and then they wake up to find they have a best-seller, such as *Atomic Energy for Military Purposes* or *The Encyclopedia of Poetry and Poetics*, which Herbert Bailey instigated. Yet I confess I am disappointed when I see a university press act as if its mission were primarily moneymaking. This is made plain when it starts to publish nonscholarly works, books certain to be published in any event. That certainty no longer holds for poetry—or short stories—so let the presses publish them. But now a good many presses compete in the trade field with commercial publishers, and though I would draw the demarcation line very generously in favor of the university presses, I hope that they will resist commercial enticements to stray away from their scholarly responsibilities.

Scribner
Reference Books

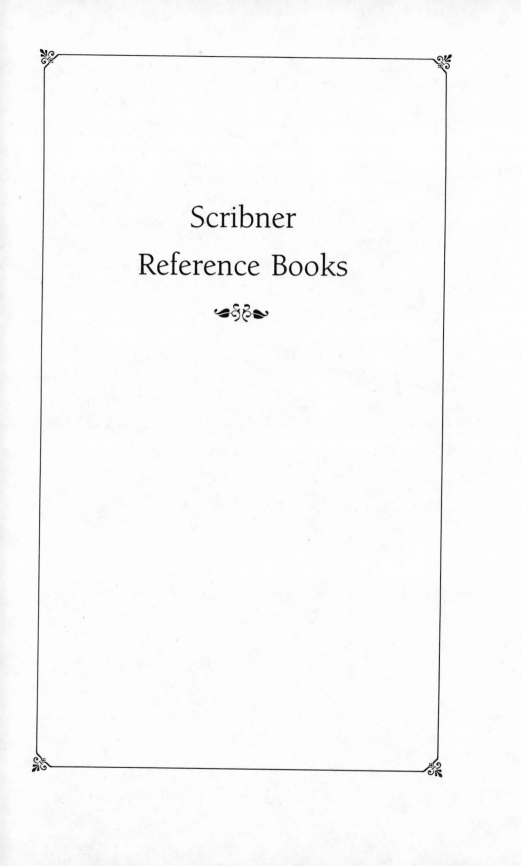

Scribners entered the field of reference books in my great-grandfather's time, when the firm published a huge biblical commentary by a man named Lange; it was a translation from the German. In the late nineteenth century, it was Scribner & Company that published in this country the ninth edition of the *Encyclopaedia Britannica*. The company was delighted with the market it reached by its vigorous sales effort; it was said that if all the volumes of the encyclopedia it had sold were put end to end, they would reach from New York to Omaha. I'm not prepared to do the work of verifying the arithmetic but I am impressed. (Alas, by the next edition, the *Britannica* had eluded our embrace and ventured out on its own.)

After the First World War, the historian and educator J. Franklin Jameson, a founder of the American Council of Learned Societies, decided that the United States should possess an equivalent of the English *Dictionary of National Biography*. Since Jameson had been involved in the Scribners series Narratives of Early American History, it was logical that he should want us to undertake his ambitious national biography project.

It was a mighty enterprise, achieved with the cooperation of all the leading American historians. The entire twenty volumes were published by the end of the 1930s, and I am glad to think that my grandfather lived to see the first couple of volumes. The family has always been proud not only of having done the *Dictionary of American Biography*, but of keeping it up to date by supplements to the present day. It is a major humanistic and historical contribution to American thought and culture. Indeed, my father used to say that the *DAB* was without question Scribners' most important work.

The dedication to American history, begun on a large scale with the *DAB*, continued thanks to the imaginative efforts of James Truslow Adams, the stockbroker-turned-scholar who coined the phrase "the American dream." It was his idea to produce a *Dictionary of American History* as a companion to the *DAB*. The work was to consist of small essays rather than standard encyclopedia entries. With it, he conceived an *Album of American History*, which would give some of the iconography of American history from the colonial period to the present. Here again was a multivolume work that we kept up to date with additional volumes.

From the start, I never had any doubt that our reference books were bright jewels in our crown, but I had no part in their editing or production until after my father died. At that time the head of the Council of Learned Societies was Professor Peter Odegard, and he was keen about bringing the *DAB* up to date by means of a supplement. Producing that first and subsequent supplements was not easy. By then, the sales of the main set brought in only modest returns and the investment needed for a regular new series was large—and not recoverable for several years. Fortunately, Whitney Oates was on the ACLS grants committee and put through a subsidy for the editorial preparation of the first supplement.

A casual encounter at a meeting of the American Library Association in San Francisco reinforced my interest in reference books. Our booth was next to Macmillan's, and one of their representatives came over to look at our display of the *Album of American History* and the *Dictionary of American History*. After gazing and hefting he said: "Look here. You've got some pretty hot stuff there. How would you like us to distribute them for you?"

I was stung. I took his "offer" to mean we weren't doing a proper job. I thereupon resolved to redouble our efforts to promote the *DAB* and its companion works. I put all my energy into it, and as a result reference books became my permanent, not to say, predominant concern. Never underestimate the power of a snub.

Our reference books were sold by a separate, noncommission sales force, independent of the trade contingent. They were not employees but free-lance soldiers. Once my father asked one of them, "How long have you worked for the company?" And the old codger replied, "A lot longer than you have."

Making reference-book publishing a main division of the firm came about logically and naturally when I began to find that trade books of "our" kind were getting difficult to acquire, for the reasons I have recounted—mainly, the agents' demand for huge advances on speculative projects. It was foolish and inefficient to wait for authors to come to us, as if we were an organism on a rock, waiting for nourishment to float by. I preferred to develop the kind of books I wanted.

As I have remarked more than once, the history of science has been a lifelong interest of mine. With that subject rattling around in my head, I went down to Princeton to call on my friend Charles Gillispie, an eminent specialist in that field. I had first come across Gillispie when I was in Washington and read his book *The Edge of Objectivity*. During that later visit I asked him how and where I could find books on the history of science to publish. His reply was: "You don't quite understand the academic world. Scholars have their own objectives, their own ideas of what's important. It's very unlikely that they would want to drop what they are doing to write the kind of book you would want to publish."

These words were plain common sense as soon as one reflected on the matter; they were also cold water thrown on my hopes. But I continued mulling over the great subject I cared about and the lack of readable books about it. Then the "Eureka" moment came. I was thinking about the *DAB* and our growing specialization in reference books. I wanted to publish more of them and I was keen on the history of science. "Why not a *DAB* in science?" Immediately I saw how it could be done. For I should have said earlier that at the time I speak of, the history of science was only just getting to be accepted as a discipline and a department of academic institutions. We would corral the scholars who were developing the new field and have them write up the lives and works of the world's notable scientists.

I went down to Princeton again to see Gillispie and told him my idea for a new, unheard-of reference work all about science, modeled on the *DAB*. It would be planned and supervised by an editorial board of scholars in the different branches of science. He said, "It's a wonderful idea, and I'd like to help you do it"—the most positive thing anyone could have said.

At yet another meeting with Gillispie and another prominent historian of science, Marshall Clagett, we discussed such difficulties as inducing scholars to do the work, enforcing deadlines, and controlling length of articles, style, and so on. Suddenly, Marshall Clagett asked me, "Charlie, you're going to do this, anyway, aren't you, whether anybody cooperates or not?" Without a moment's thought I said,

"Yes, I am." From his look I could see I had the project off to a good start.

Following the model of the *DAB* in another sense, we decided that we should try to obtain the sponsorship of the American Council of Learned Societies. Frederick Burkhardt was then the director; he was a philosopher and his interest was at once aroused. He gathered the panjandrums in the history of science at a luncheon in New York—Clagett, Gillispie, Bernard Cohen, and others—to consult them about the merits of the idea.

They cheered it, and decided to make it a project of the History of Science Society, a component of the ACLS. Through this linkage the ACLS would take it under its wing in the same way that it had taken the *DAB*. Burkhardt went down to Washington and got the biggest publication grant that the National Science Foundation and the National Endowment for the Humanities had ever awarded. From then on, the *DSB* was certain to come into being.

But for me one uncertainty remained. The terms of the grant required that the project be put out for bids. I found myself like a surrogate mother, wondering whether my brainchild would be removed from me forever: we might not be able to meet the bid of another company. The sizable subvention from the National Science Foundation made it possible to turn in a very good offer and so we got the book.

The next step was to set up shop at Scribners: an office for Gillispie, to which he came frequently for his work with the team of editors from our firm; and the machinery for editorial meetings where we thrashed out the successive principles and policies. It was an exciting half dozen years. The revelation had come in 1963; the first volume appeared in 1970.

My direct participation in the making was a foregone conclusion. With the help of a French work on the history of science, I drew up a first list of eligible subjects. I put a dot opposite every name in the index that I thought at least deserving of consideration, and I had a young assistant type it for me. By a series of small mistakes this purely clerical phase had an amusing result: Isaac Newton was left out of the preliminary list. I have suspected ever since that one or two of the eminent scholars rather distrusted my judgment after that. But what a curious chance that instead of one of the expendables Newton should be the name to fall out!

The editorial meetings were to me a source of great satisfaction, both because the work was going forward smoothly and because, in spite of my lack of formal qualifications, I was treated as a colleague. I made suggestions, even particular suggestions about some of the men of science and their work, all of which were received with great politeness. Indeed, I was detailed to work on a few of the entries, and toward the end wrote part of the article on Einstein and special relativity.

Just as Scribners had produced a *Concise DAB*, we decided to "concise" the *DSB*. I assigned myself the articles on George Boole and Niels Bohr and discovered in the process what an excellent self-teaching operation it is to boil down information to its essentials.

Indexing was a mammoth undertaking. At Gillispie's suggestion, we began by approaching IBM to find out if they could facilitate the work. They could not. Computerized publishing was not far enough advanced; there was no use in mere automation. Take, for example, the word *gravity*. It will occur at the point where the article speaks of the propounder of universal gravitation and it will occur again in the statement "Newton's character was marked by great personal gravity." Only a human being can separate these two uses of one word. The index therefore required a great deal of human brain work.

This work was carried out by a young woman in North Carolina named Julie McVaugh, who led a team of trained assistants. The task was time-consuming and enormously expensive. When done, the index, which filled a large number of boxes, was brought to New York in a station wagon. Today it would all be on computer tapes.

The index to the *DSB* is of course a most important part of its value. With such an index, ideas, names, and formulas are juxtaposed as they have probably never been juxtaposed before. The relations thus brought out now stood out clearly for the first time. For the scholar this was the great heuristic value of the index, on top of its practical utility in locating the wanted fact.

Indexing takes a human mind, and one both trained and familiar with the subject, so as to recognize ideas that are not expressly stated in words. For example, the use of *invariance* in mathematics may occur in a discussion even though the word *invariant* is nowhere mentioned. The indexer must seize on the allusion or, if careless or ignorant, pass by an important reference to invariance.

My work with Gillispie had for me an unexpected consequence. I was emboldened to write an article for the *American Journal of Physics*. I first submitted it to his judgment and then to other physicists at Princeton. They were all encouraging and the upshot was the publication of a paper in their professional journal of a piece by someone who never even took a college course in physics.

The article, entitled "Poincaré and the Principle of Relativity," was an attempt to disentangle the role Poincaré played in the development of the theory of relativity and the application of relativity to the electrodynamics of moving bodies. The point of the article was to locate the gap in theory that Einstein had bridged by his epoch-making contribution. Any such gap in science, or any other field, is the locus of the next major achievement. Investigating the Poincaré-Einstein situation deepened my understanding of how science progresses and in my own eyes seemed both to set the seal on my delvings into the history of science and to qualify me, ex post facto, as the publisher of the *DSB*.

As editor-in-chief, Gillispie was a scholar's scholar, uncompromising and tireless. He read every article in the fifteen volumes. Sometimes he had to translate pieces from other languages; he had no trouble with French, but occasionally he and I had to struggle with German.

A more annoying editorial difficulty arose out of the contributions by the Soviet authors. They gave us lifeless stuff, impossibly written. Had we been wiser, we would not have made a contract for their participation. They could not refrain from mixing politics with their science. The numerous physicists, mathematicians, chemists, and astronomers who disappeared in Stalin's era had to be mentioned or given an entry, and that created embarrassment for our Soviet contributors. Worse still was their refusal to cooperate unless Marx and Lenin were represented in the *DSB* as scientists. Marx barely qualified as having had some influence on the subject, but Lenin had only negative qualifications. He thought of science as wholly derived from dialectical materialism, and he denied Einstein's relativity theory as an erroneous product of bourgeois thought.

I wished we could make the *DSB* complete without Russian help, though I saw that Gillispie had made his pact with them in the best interests of the work. I suppose we were lucky not to be asked to include an entry on Stalin. Near the end we got a cable, "We send you our tanks," which we thought an ominous misprint.

Our other foreign editors enabled us to strike the right balance in assigning space and importance and of course to get the best authority to write entries. We had some surprises. It seemed that a most outstanding French scientist, Laplace, had had virtually nothing written about him. When Gillispie went to the Bibliothèque Nationale to investigate, he was confidently misdirected to *Lagrange*! This lacuna was a scandal. The *DSB* article on Laplace was written almost entirely by Gillispie himself, a piece of original scholarship in every sense. I have had the good fortune to keep up my friendship with Gillispie and see him at meetings of the American Philosophical Society. Among other things, we discuss the latest news about the history of science—or Princeton.

One incident of more than passing significance occurred in connection with the symbol I chose for the set—a little wreath of spheres. I thought it appropriate because it symbolized the two sides of science, experiment and "thought," which we call theory. The drawing used was taken from a scientist named Simon Stevinus, who made it to represent the composition of forces on an inclined plane. With this colophon, it seemed to me, we should give an explanation of what it meant and how it exemplified scientific work.

So I wrote a brief account of what Stevinus had discovered. More astonishing as a discovery was that nobody could get our consultant scientists to agree on a simple one-paragraph description of Stevinus's experiment. So we never supplied one. I had planned to put symbol and explanation at the back of the book, but "*les savants ne voulaient rien savoir.*" That experience taught me a new principle of scholarly behavior: "The academic mind is filled with alternatives."

Besides an editor, a publication needs a copy editor, and a work such as the *DSB* needs not one but a team, headed by a captain. We appointed Marshall De Bruhl to that post as managing editor, because he had been trained at Macmillan by Jean Paradise and was experienced in running such a group. He applied the Paradise standards that had been adopted throughout publishing and taught us to worship at the altar of the *Chicago Manual of Style.*

One of the facts the copy editors had to verify was whether a given scientist was really dead. Nobody could get into the *DSB* alive. The matter was not always easy to ascertain. About some, false ideas were afloat of their dying or living, and our delvings turned up many misconceptions current up to that time. On one occasion I wanted to quote General David Sarnoff, who had said at a meeting of publishers that more candles were being sold in the United States than a hundred years earlier. He meant to cheer up those of us who sold objects as antiquated as candles. In quoting the quip, I did not know whether or not to say "the *late* General Sarnoff." I called RCA and said, "I'm terribly embarrassed but can you tell me whether General Sarnoff is still alive?" The receptionist replied, "Just a minute, I'll call his secretary." In another instance, we asked Dame Kathleen Lonsdale, the chemist, to write the entry on her colleague Ralph Wyckoff. Researching Wyckoff, we found out that he was still alive, so we wrote to cancel her assignment. In the meantime she had died, so instead we asked Wyckoff to do the piece on her.

Some time after the event, Gillispie assured me that the publication of the *DSB* established the history of science as a discipline by giving it "a local habitation and a name." Anybody who wants to know what the history of science is can turn to fifteen volumes of evidence. "*Si monumentum requiris circumspice.*"

But why need science bother about its history? Only the latest science has validity for the world and interest for scientists. The answer is, the history of science is one of the humanities and as such it matters to all human beings who think about their place and fate in the universe. In the introduction to the *DSB,* Gillispie wrote, "The history of science is made by men and not by themes or abstractions." That sums up the humanistic importance both of the *DSB* and of its bearing.

Take the *DSB* article on Einstein as an illustration. It is a study of Einstein as a man at work on a problem. It tells who his precursors were, what the problem was, how he met it, how he was influenced by other people, not only in science but in the whole realm of the life of the mind. To put it another way, scientific work does not take place in a vacuum. Once you realize that fact your view of the humanities and humanistic education will broaden immeasurably. Wherever a department of knowledge deals with creativity, it must deal with the creator and with his surroundings and his interpreters—those who fought or helped or exploited him for good or ill. That is the reason why it is unwise to separate the humanities and the sciences between different curricula. The sciences and the humanities are but different perspectives on one central subject matter—man and his works.

Accordingly, I don't think humanists need to be in retreat. And by the same token, I feel free to claim that all of the reference books I have sponsored are humanistic, whatever branch of knowledge they cover. One practical problem remains as to their use. Although we had quite a few private subscribers to the *DSB*, it is difficult to get these reference books sold to individuals—how to get the oats to the horses? There must be thousands of individuals who would love to have a set of the *DSB*. Frank Sinatra subscribed, for one, and I have struggled for years to figure out a way to find others. Our sales are 99.9 percent to institutions. There are technical obstacles about discounts and the habits of book buyers and booksellers. The sets are expensive, and short of a special force of door-to-door salesmen such as encyclopedias employ, the obstacle remains insurmountable.

The *Dictionary of Scientific Biography* became the cornerstone of our expanding program of reference-book publishing. Just as the *DAB* had its natural offspring, the *DSB* generated the several volumes of our *Album of Science*. At that point, I conceived what may qualify as a new idea—the "reading reference book." That might be defined as works covering a large subject in one or more volumes that can be used to find basic information by consulting the index, and that can also be read like a series of introductions to the subject's constituent parts.

The first reference work of this type after the *DSB* was the five-volume *Dictionary of the History of Ideas*. Its plan was more complicated, because the *DSB* was a plain parallel to the *DAB* —a set of biographies short or long. Ideas cannot be arranged in that simple way. In devising the needed scheme, I was influenced by Arthur Lovejoy's *The Great Chain of Being* and his *Documentary History of Primitivism and Related Ideas in Antiquity*, which I had read when I was at Princeton.

From Lovejoy I learned that many contemporary ideas probably were the transmutation of previous ideas, not necessarily recent. It might therefore be possible to produce a work about ideas on a pattern resembling that of chemistry, an idea being conceived of as a molecule made up of a number of different molecules. Transformations in the course of time could be seen as recombinations of these atomic constituents into different units with new properties and powers. A book composed on this principle would be at once instructive and truly philosophical.

Although the editorial board adopted the idea, the contributors could not be induced to stick to it. It wasn't workable on the practical plane of expectation and response. Nonetheless, our interesting and useful reference book was produced. Certain ideas, such as Freedom and Religion, by their very nature caused the writers to follow my proposed scheme. But I was disappointed that the other philosophers didn't want to be philosophical.

The work was a great success. In the quality paperback edition, the Book-of-the-Month Club sold tens of thousands of sets. From an economic point of view, "mere ideas" paid off. They still sell, and perhaps the work should be brought up to date, but what I viewed as its birth defects has kept me from wanting to do anything more with it. I had many other more attractive subjects to pursue—such as world history.

In creating reference works about history, we chose to break up the field into separate projects rather than attempt a unified treatment. It would have run to a prohibitive number of volumes and the amount of capital to be invested long before returns would have been huge. Instead, I developed for all our reference works what I might call a modular design. For example, in tackling the history of the ancient Mediterranean and its prolongation into the Middle Ages, we divided the span, the events, into self-contained blocks. In this great cathedral that we wanted to build, the Middle Ages would rise in the center and would be topped by a series of volumes on Modern European history. That is, the *Dictionary of the Middle Ages* would appear as if it were a set in itself, but in my mind it was from the start but one segment of a continuum.

The plan has worked well. Librarians have been patient and not only accepted our reference works in sets of three or four volumes, but as in the *Dictionary of the Middle Ages*, which is in twelve, they have got used to receiving them one volume at a time. No doubt they had learned from their purchase of the *DSB*, which also came out in separate volumes, that we pushed to the end and did not leave them with only half an alphabet of names.

On the *Dictionary of the Middle Ages* we lavished design and decoration to make it beautiful. Each volume has a frontispiece appropriate to the first article. Aristotle faces the scholars of antiquity; other volumes show the Bayeux Tapestry in full color, or the choir of Chartres.

Our reference works overlap at some points, necessarily. For example, we have an article on Thomas Aquinas in the *Dictionary of Scientific Biography*, because of his scientific influence; another in the *Dictionary of the History of Ideas*; and a third in the *Dictionary of the Middle Ages*. The remarkable thing is that reading all three does not give one the sense of redundancy. As all these sets began to form a library, I became more and more convinced that the scheme had its own destiny independent of my will. Our responsibility as publishers was to fulfill the purpose I had conceived—to supply sourcebooks devoted to the pedagogy of the humanities.

Through the right mixture of intention and the turn of fortune's wheel, we had created a new type of book, the reading-reference work. I don't believe the innovative element is as yet generally appreciated, except in professional circles. The form is simple: separate essays are written by specialists who know how to write for the student or general reader. These essays are carefully edited, verified as to fact, purged of bias if necessary. Each constitutes a "port of entry" into the particular topic. Taken together in one volume or as one set, they cover the designated field of study. The result is a tremendous pedagogical thrust—readable scholarship made available to both the young learner and the intelligent layman. At the same time, I think these books have given renewed life to the essay form, each a comprehensive treatment, fifteen thousand words long, with a beginning, a middle, and an end. Though I'm proud of the reading-reference work, I do not lay claim to the concept; rather, I feel that like all valuable inventions, it invented itself.

*　　　　*　　　　*

As a boy at school, in the middle of the Depression of the 1930s, I was fascinated by the Haldeman-Julius blue books. They were little three-by-five pamphlets of eight or sixteen pages held together with one little piece of thread down the middle. They cost five cents apiece and were advertised in the newspapers in a huge list of hundreds of titles. Most were biographies or philosophical essays; some were on sociology, including a few mildly risqué subjects such as prostitution. Boarding-school customers were then so susceptible to anything that spoke of sex that those daring titles had enormous appeal. As literature, these little books were of good quality. Bertrand Russell wrote on philosophy, Tolstoy on religion, and so on. The article on Haldeman-Julius in the *Dictionary of American Biography* truthfully records his influence on American life.

The point of this reminiscence is to prove once again that chance favors the prepared mind, as Pasteur said. When Leon Shimkin was working for Simon & Schuster, he got the idea of putting the Haldeman-Julius pieces on philosophy, many of which were written by Will Durant, into a single volume. It was called *The Story of Philosophy*, and beginning in 1926 it became one of the best-sellers of American publishing. From time to time I hoped that someday my prepared mind might seize on a comparable idea.

Sure enough, through reading an essay by Louis Auchincloss on Edith Wharton, I ran across a series called the University of Minnesota Pamphlets. The Wharton pamphlet was sent to me probably because of a permission requirement. It looked attractive, inside and out. Of course, Louis Auchincloss writes like an angel and is an old friend besides. The next time I saw him, I said, "I read the piece you did for the Minnesota Pamphlets. Are they all as good?" He said, "Yes, they are very well written and edited." I ordered a complete set, read through them, and got Jacques Barzun to read some; they were indeed excellent. I got in touch with the University of Minnesota Press and asked if we might publish their pamphlets in volume form. Their reply was, "Yes, we can make an arrangement, but you're crazy, they have only a small sale, even though the price is only fifty cents." I knew they would sell very much better brought together in one volume. We published it as *American Writers*, and it was a runaway success.

We went on to do *British Writers*. The British Council, organized for cultural propaganda, had a series of pamphlets called *Writers and Their Work*, which was in fact the model for Minnesota's. The editorial head in England was a scholar named Ian Scott-Kilvert, a distinguished classicist. I called on him and we arranged with the council to collect and reissue them. But they needed a good deal of work first. Again, Jacques Barzun read the 150 or so, editing and singling out those that needed redoing entirely. The set of seven volumes plus a later supplement are still selling.

After that there was no stopping us. We put together a volume on writers for children, three volumes on Shakespeare, and went on to take up the Continental European writers. George Stade of Columbia University was the editor-in-chief. That set carried the history of literature from the Middle Ages to the present day, and finally we invited T. James Luce of Princeton to edit two volumes of similar essays entitled *Ancient Writers*. It sold fully as well as the preceding sets, and all met with critical approval.

I might add that when I asked Professor Luce, the head of the Classics Department at Princeton, to undertake the job, I told him I wanted these reading-reference books to be "essentially propaedeutic." He complied, but tacked on a little note at the end: "Charlie Scribner wanted to have these essays propaedeutic; I also wanted them to be protreptic." It was a little skirmish between students of Greek. It took me about an hour to find *protreptic* in the Liddell & Scott dictionary, because my Greek is somewhat substandard. It turned out that *protreptic* is equivalent to *hortatory* in Latin, so Luce means this work to be "encouraging," urging readers to go on.

The assumption is that a student who reads the section on Tacitus, for example, starts as one who knows nothing about Tacitus, and may not ever read anything about Tacitus again. His fund of knowledge comes from that essay, and that is what creates for the writer of the essay his problem in pedagogy. What do you tell the student that is really worth knowing? Solving this propaedeutic exercise is one of the reasons for the success of our reference works: they are propaedeutic and protreptic, and for all I know prophylactic, too. And for the ambitious who will go on, they contain an up-to-date bibliography.

In planning our publishing program, we start with a bridgehead of one work on an established subject, and if it is successful, we expand the bridgehead over neighboring fields until it covers the whole continent. It's the sensible way to proceed; we do not commit all our troops at once, but only as the way opens, and then fulfill the "entelechy" of that particular idea. I confess I relish this notion of entelechy—of destiny. We used it in an ad detailing "the entelechy of our reference books." It appeared in the library media and their readers took to it. So I went on to play with other Greek words, like *pempte ousia*, which is "the fifth substance"—the *quintessence*. I thought teaching the librarians a little Greek would not impair their efficiency.

At one of the meetings of the American Philosophical Society that I attended I heard a paper entitled "Jefferson as an Architect." It was so engaging that it inspired me to do a reference book entirely devoted to Jefferson—every aspect of his life, his work, his genius, his friends. Thus *Thomas*

Jefferson: A Reference Biography, consisting of some two dozen essays on as many aspects, came into existence. Its editor, recommended to me by Arthur Link, the editor of the Woodrow Wilson Papers, was Merrill Peterson of the University of Virginia. He did a beautiful job, but the book was not a success.

In a postmortem session we surmised that libraries already owned many books on Jefferson and did not need another. They were probably buying each volume of the Dumas Malone biography as it came out and did not need an expensive single-volume reference book.

It had one unusual feature. In my father's desk I found after his death a little leather case containing a copperplate engraving. I didn't at first know what it was, but discovered by chance it was a portrait of Jefferson, made by an itinerant artist named Saint-Memin using the so-called physiotrace method. Investigating further, I found that my little copperplate was Jefferson's own copy. It had been purchased by my grandfather after the Civil War. I put a replica of it on the jacket of the book, thus adding (I hoped) another element of interest to the work.

On the other hand, a comparable work, *The Presidents*, was a great success and sold many copies. Professor Henry F. Graff of Columbia chose the ranking experts who would each write an essay on one President—not just the men themselves, but their administrations and the way they found and left the office of Chief Executive.

At the time of publication, a trip to the White House was indicated, so that we might present a copy of the book to the incumbent. President Reagan received the editor and me in the Oval Office—my first visit there and, I daresay, my last. It was an amusing occasion; the President was not at all solemn or distant. "Mr. Scribner," he asked, "is the present administration included in your book?" (It was the middle of his first term.) I replied, "No, Mr. President, you won't be in it until the conclusion of your second term." He laughed and said, "Oh, you're counting on a second term, are you?" "Yes," I said.

My visit to the White House made me the third-generation Scribner to be received there. My grandfather was a close friend of Theodore Roosevelt, all of whose works we published. It was on that account that my grandfather visited what was then called the Executive Mansion. I think he was a little bit disillusioned by Roosevelt as a person, although Roosevelt was a great man of letters and a great President. But he was also a great show-stealer, and I think my grandfather was dismayed to find him so much of an egotist.

My father's visit to the White House took place when Hoover was President. Scribners had published *Addresses on the American Road*, a collection of Hoover's speeches. It was not a best-seller; nor was his subsequent collection of addresses to the Gridiron Club, *Hoover After Dinner*.

The work we published in 1988 entitled the *Encyclopedia of Asian History* prompts me to reflect again on chance and the prepared mind. Datus Smith, the former director of the Princeton University Press, served at one time as assistant to John D. Rockefeller III, and in that capacity worked with us on the preparation of a book on the Rockefeller family. John D. III was always interested in Asian history and wanted to have somebody prepare material for the high schools of the United States, so that students might learn about the subject. He wanted to publish it in pamphlet form. In the spirit of Scribner publishing, I said, "No pamphlets." To make a mark on the country as a whole, nothing less will do than a reference set for libraries—for high school libraries particularly. Pamphlets are lost or thrown away.

Books are permanent and serve generations. I told Datus, "Please do it that way."

They agreed, a little grudgingly. It took three or four volumes to do it and quite a slice of time. Yet I believe this set may be one of the most influential of our reference books, because there is such a lack and such a need in our understanding of the Asian world. From the standpoint of our Scribner Reference Library, this title fills a great space in our offering on world history. It takes Asian history from Darius and Cyrus right through to the present day.

Scribners had a marketing and sales department for reference books before my ideas on the subject took shape. In fact, that earlier tradition was the *sine qua non* of my success. A publisher cannot succeed with reference books for libraries without a sales force that builds up its credentials with librarians. Our field force was in being but needed some invigoration. We needed to sell the supplements to the *DAB*, and the first thing I pushed was the regular production and marketing of these supplements.

We had practically nothing else to offer in that line except some books by James Truslow Adams and the original volumes of the *Dictionary of American Biography*. These were known as "subscription books," because they were sold on subscription by salesmen traveling around the country. The subscription department needed life pumped into it, as well as new books. With that in view, my cousin George Schieffelin and I brought in a live wire named Jack Galazka. He took charge of the division and made it over. We soon wouldn't have had any reference department if he hadn't kept it going by sheer grit and brains.

Jack was also a marvelous scout, finding new books in all sorts of fields that were not fashionable on the New York publishing scene—books on medicine, gardening, farming, art, home crafts, and so on. He diversified our bill of fare, and he was not only shrewd but cautious. I had told him what Thomas Y. Crowell had told me. Crowell had a strong list of reference works, and he likened publishing them to being a piano mover: it's good going until you drop your first piano. I took that seriously. At worst, I have dropped an accordion.

In the original *Dictionary of American Biography* there are some serious omissions. It was the work of scholars who shaped it according to the lights of their time. There was then no "business history" to speak of, so industrialists were neglected. So were women and artists, as well as Indian chieftains and members of other ethnic groups. The supplements have remedied these defects but only for their own time span. Something needs doing to the original set.

I wanted to perform that task by issuing a retrospective *DAB* in one or more volumes devoted to the neglected figures. New information, if any, about those already in could also be added. I think this supplementation is the thrifty and the sensible way to handle the situation—thrifty from the standpoint of whoever undertakes the publication and also thrifty from the standpoint of whoever has to buy the work.

It seems, however, that Oxford University Press has obtained a contract from the American Council of Learned Societies to do a new national biography from scratch. Knowing the scope of such an effort—getting it written, edited, and produced; keeping it up to date by supplements; and keeping the ever-growing set in print—I have grave doubts of the wisdom of doing the basic work all over again.

Think of the very large number of persons already written up—settlers, explorers, writers, clergymen, pioneers, scientists, politicians, baseball players, even publishers, about whom there is nothing more to be said or to be found out.

They matter to the history of the country, but they need no reinterpretation. Their "lives," long or short, were written by scholars and stand there in definitive print in the first twenty volumes. To do them over in different words seems sheer waste.

Be that as it may, the happiness and pride that our Reference Library has given me must be apparent. It has led me into all kinds of pleasant places and interesting connections, such as my membership in the American Philosophical Society. It's gratifying to have success with books and make money from it, but it is a more lasting pleasure to think that what one publishes may enrich the contents of American education and cultural literacy at all levels.

Writers and Friends

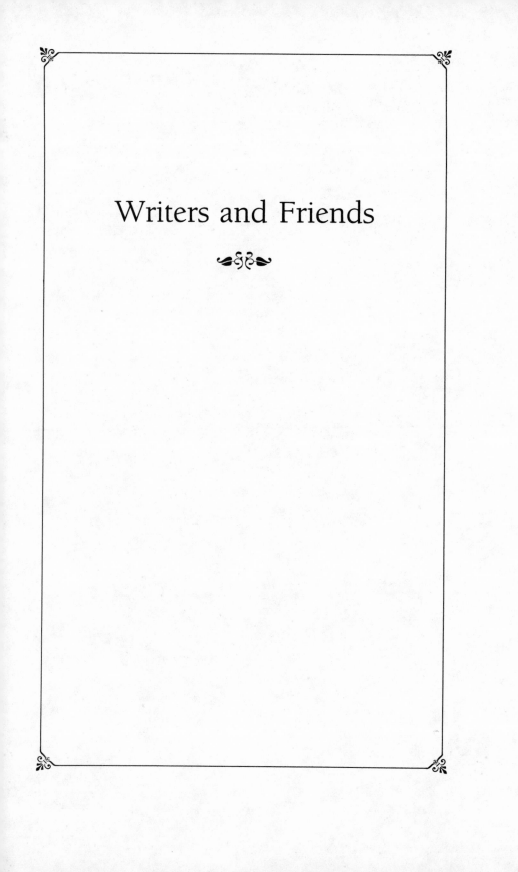

The firm keeps a copyright book in which we list information about all the books that we have published. I used to go through the copyright book and to my surprise found that I could remember something about every book published during my tenure of office, and even about a few before that time. These memories are fading now. Of course, I was only able to read a small number of those books before publication, but I managed to learn something about each. I read everything we did in the realm of science, many children's books, and most of the detective stories. About the authors, I kept myself *au courant* and became close to a good many of them. I made a point of knowing our education authors, our college text authors, and naturally all our outstanding authors. I would have scorned the role of absentee, know-nothing publisher.

C. P. Snow was in his time a highly regarded novelist; his views on science, society, government, and literature had considerable influence; he invented the concept of "the two cultures." I first got to know him when he left his first American publisher and Burroughs Mitchell acquired the rights to *The New Men* on one of his trips to England. That novel was about the making of the atomic bomb. Lewis Eliot, the protagonist of Snow's series of novels, *Strangers and Brothers*, gets involved in a secret Oak Ridge sort of project with political and moral implications. Snow was ostensibly a left-wing writer, but as I came to know him I discovered that in his heart of hearts his radical stances were more ritualistic than passionate.

Snow next came out with a tremendous best-seller called *The Affair*. It was a Book-of-the-Month Club selection, and at the launching that the club hosted, Snow was gracious toward our firm—and the nation. He said, "I'm thankful to Charlie for having made my fortune in America." From then on, we had a most enjoyable friendship. Joan and I visited him and his wife, Pamela Hansford Johnson, also a novelist, in their home, and we published her books as well. *A Humbler Creation*, an early book of hers, was a splendid achievement, although we weren't lucky enough to have published it.

Snow probably got more American honorary degrees than any man in history. His idea of the two cultures, the literary and the scientific, set forth in a 1959 essay, stressed the revelation of the age, and in virtually every state of the Union, some institution took note of it by asking him to speak and draping another hood over his head. Sir Charles was very pro-American and especially admiring of the American educational system, which he saw as the instrument of upward mobility and more effective than the English.

He was one of our steadiest backlist authors until his literary reputation was maimed by the devastating attack of the English critic F. R. Leavis. In essence, Leavis said that Snow didn't know much about science and knew even less about literature. Snow was pulling too long a bow for his limited intellectual strength. It was a violent, rather mean-spirited onslaught, which proved the turning point in Snow's career. His sales went down almost at once. His fashionableness among the intelligentsia leaked away and he never recovered status.

Snow had a kindly, warm personality, and a good sense of humor. He was gregarious and very sharp about people. One can read about him in a book written by a friend, William Cooper's *Scenes from Provincial Life*, where Snow figures as a character. I think it was Rudolph Peierls, the English physicist, who told me about Snow's recruitment of scientists for the war effort. Snow's ability to judge a candidate's capacity was uncanny: without tests or tables—or résumés—Snow could tell whether or not a man packed a wallop intellectually.

Snow was a poor boy born in Leicester who came up through the ranks educationally by sheer intelligence and determination. Some of that native cunning that poor people acquire for judging others was obviously powerful in him. Wealth and power fascinated him. In view of his left-wing sympathies, it was ironic to notice how overawed he was by the mighty in the corridors of power. He had been knighted for his war services; eventually he was made a life peer. One day when we were having lunch, he said to me, "I met Lord So-and-So in the House, and we talked about various matters. The extraordinary thing, though, was that he just didn't give a damn." Snow's attitude struck me as incongruous for a man who *did* give a damn. Here he was, bowled over like a schoolboy by the charm of somebody not half as responsible morally as himself.

We referred to him affectionately as His Lordship. Under all the heavy *Wissenschaftlichkeit* and advanced ideas, here was a young man, very ambitious, deeply impressed by power, and boyishly pleased by the shower of awards and acclaim he received. His astuteness was genuine, but underneath he lived his life as a romance and saw everything else in the same way. That was his charm.

Although his wife was a fine writer—finer than he—she was self-abnegating when in public with him. She seemed quiet and shy, but had a strong character, too. They were obviously a very compatible couple. They would laugh in unison at many things and they could both be funny; they were a team. When I first knew them they lived in the Cromwell Road, in a rather dilapidated flat. With affluence and reputation assured, they moved to a house in Eaton Terrace. The new surroundings supplied the atmosphere in Snow's second book of crime fiction, *A Coat of Varnish*, published in 1979, a year before his death, and almost a half-century after his first novel, also a murder mystery, *Death Under Sail*—two unexpected brackets for a rich life in letters.

Scribners owed its connection with Loren Eiseley to the science editor Kenneth Heuer. Eiseley was a strange man, whom people were quickly tempted to call "poetic." His mother had been deaf and that had affected him in peculiar ways. He was haunted by death. One time he went with a friend to a cemetery where he had taken a plot. When he saw the actual place, he lay down and stretched out on the ground in which his grave would be dug. As a young man he rode the rails for quite a while and saw a lot of the country, before ending up as author, man of science, professor, and high official in the administration of the University of Pennsylvania.

Comparisons suggest themselves when one thinks of Loren Eiseley and C. P. Snow together. Eiseley also lived life as a romance and found inspiration in science. His lyrical prose dealt with ideas based on his knowledge of biology. Oddly enough, in speech he often defied grammar and coherence, which was never true of Snow. One day at lunch Loren and I had a long and interesting talk in which he went on uttering like a machine. At the end he said, "You know, it's simply great the way that we have gotten to know each other today—it means a lot to me." I said good-bye as we parted and he said, "Good-bye, Harry."

Eiseley's vision of nature and life was extraordinary, unique to himself. He would retell stories of the sphinx wasps that paralyze insects and store them for their own larvae to eat when they grow up. In Eiseley's ornate prose this prudent practice would sound gruesome, frightening, macabre; the scene suggested an ancient Roman prison and torture chamber. His mind was dominated by a literary sense of evil in the manner of Poe. Eiseley's books didn't take the world by storm, but they sold well. Among his readers, W. H. Auden was a great admirer, and Auden's praise is something to note.

When my son Charlie was a boy of seventeen, he and I went to England together, and on that occasion I remember meeting P. D. James for the first time. The three of us had dinner at the Hyde Park Hotel, and we hit it off immediately. We were good friends at once. Ever after, no visit to England in later years was thinkable without an evening with Phyllis. We published her, of course, but seeing her was for pleasure. Conversation with her was entertainment in itself.

Appreciating her personality led me to bring her over to visit the United States in 1975. Two years later our publicity director, Susan Richman, insisted she return for a major media tour. It had a marked effect on her career and established her reputation in this country as a leader in her genre, the classic English detective novel, and ultimately as a novelist who transcended the genre.

Her husband, a physician, had been badly injured in the war and hospitalized for a long time. They had two daughters whom she raised while she worked in the Forensic

Department of the Home Office. When she decided to try her hand at crime fiction, she had the advantage of being able to portray a professional detective out of firsthand knowledge. Most of her predecessors, such as Dorothy Sayers, had had to make do with amateur detectives, for want of knowing the ropes. P. D. James was the professional's professional. Her detective, Adam Dalgliesh, is an expert in his field, although also keen about literature and a published poet to boot.

Phyllis, too, writes poetry and is widely read. Once when she was with us in the country, I asked her if she liked Jane Austen—she seemed like an Austenite. Her reply was "Are you joking? I named my daughter Jane after you-know-who." During the London Blitz, she and her two girls spent nights in the Underground, huddled under blankets. "I never could have got through that," she said, "if it hadn't been for Jane Austen." Her admiration is doubtless due to kinship. Her warmth, her sense of humor, and not least her hardheadedness make her a natural Austenite. The very special friendship my wife, Joan, and I share with Phyllis goes far beyond the best of author-publisher associations; indeed, it has continued undimmed years after we ceased being her American publishers.

Years ago, when I was a tyro in publishing, I asked Jacques Barzun to contribute to a biographical series called The Twentieth Century Library. Jacques politely refused. He was wise, because the series was not well conceived and did not prosper. Subsequently, he and I served as joint arbitrators in a case of plagiarism, and still later, we got to really know each other through C. P. Snow. Jacques was a close friend of his, and when Snow was to give a speech at a hospital in the South Bronx (it was cheerfully labeled "For

Incurable Diseases"—not encouraging for the patients), we found ourselves seated together in the audience.

Jacques and I rode back from the talk in the bus provided for safety in that dangerous neighborhood, and we agreed in a tactful way not disloyal to our mutual friend Snow that he had not been up to par in that would-be scientific lecture. Sometime later, Jacques asked me to lunch with him and in the course of conversation told me that he was retiring from Columbia and had an idea he wanted to put to me: would I consider the possibility of his acting as literary consultant for Scribners? He said, "I think I am a proficient enough editor." That was putting it mildly. He is probably the most expert editor who has ever edited.

Many years before, the firm had included a literary adviser. I revived the post, so to speak, and asked Jacques to come in two days a week and gave him an office. It was the best thing I ever did. That was in 1975 and he is helping us still in the way we devise for the good of our projects. Besides going over with care our reference works on writers (all but the ancient classics), Jacques edited the books about music, including the technical—*The Clarinet, The Flute Book, The Orchestra*. In the same way, he took on a host of biographies, from Ellen Terry and Zola, Swift and Trollope, Madame Restell and Tolstoy to "Gyroscope" Sperry, Dorothy Sayers, and many others. Naturally, he vetted the books we did in translations from the French. It turned out, too, that he was an authority on crime fiction and he had some canny suggestions for the authors on our list. Together, he and I edited James Trefil's series of books on science for the layman, and he even helped me, by questioning and rewriting, to make completely lucid a book on the golf stroke, though he knows nothing about the game.

In time, I discovered his other blind spots—or perhaps I should say "areas of restrained enthusiasm": books about gardening, needlework, and the fighting planes of World War II. Jacques is one of the most erudite of men. He's in a class with Dr. Johnson for encyclopedic knowledge, literary taste, and common sense. It is virtually impossible to find something he doesn't know about. I am not surprised that his title as an overseas member of Cambridge University is Extraordinary Fellow.

He also knows very firmly what he believes and doesn't believe, and that was for us a great model. I mean that for me and for Scribners, one of the benefits of working with him was that his intellectual standards, his command of the literature in many fields, his grasp of pedagogy, and his philosophical view of life simply by contagion raised all our own standards. I know that by just watching him work he made me more demanding of simplicity and clarity in my writing.

He is the best editor I have ever seen—and the most efficient. He works steadily, making deft intermarginal notes that are right on target. I have not written anything in the last dozen years that Jacques didn't improve by these deft touches. I studied them to see if I could do the same for myself, but I never could. He has helped ever so many writers in that same way, and none that he has helped could ever understand the mystery of Jacques's ability to find the *mot juste* or whatever was required to clarify or simplify. He is a bewildering virtuoso.

For example, when we worked together with two authors on a book about the Rockefeller family, Jacques, with the authors' full consent, edited the huge typescript, cutting, tightening, improving every page. The authors called it "Barzunizing." These writers were not tyros, they were professionals, and they just couldn't believe what he was able to do by way of saying what *they* wanted to say. Working with him was like working with Goethe or somebody of that order. It's a chance that comes once in a lifetime.

I am sure that Jacques's being bilingual has helped to make him one of the expert users of American English. He came to the United States at the age of fourteen, speaking only French (he can still think and write in French), and I have a hunch that he made a decision then and there to speak English well. He doesn't speak it *well*; he speaks it perfectly. This influence on his mind of two complex languages is what gives his writing that little bit of superaccuracy that the French have the secret of. And yet his prose is totally American, too—with something else added.

As a professional writer, his output is incredible. It seems as if he never stopped writing. He reads a good deal (in addition to the large amount that he edits), but the wonder is when and where he finds the time to write. For he's very sociable as well—not at all *"Herr Professor."* He talks readily and pleasantly, and he has made many friends among the Scribners staff. Talking to him, you know that you're dealing with a man of powerful intellect. We have been colleagues and friends for fifteen years, and it has meant a great deal to me. I have never found a situation in which I didn't feel it wise to talk things over with him, for the sake of a new idea, a new approach, a hint about a possible danger, or opportunity.

I got to know Rudolf Bing because I wrote to him and asked if he would write a book I could publish—his memoirs as general manager of the Metropolitan Opera. Bing wrote back that he could not because he was under contract with Doubleday. But he wanted to talk about that contract and invited Joan and me to come to his box at the Met. Thereafter we went often to that box. My wife, with her natural sparkle, was undoubtedly the cause of our repeated invitations. Bing liked having her in that box—and I don't blame him. As for my advice on his contract, it was to say that I thought it a good one; Doubleday was doing right by him.

Another reason, I suspect, that we were asked back so often was that we were undemanding and even submissive guests. Being head of the opera was terribly hard on his nerves. Once, when he was putting on a new production of *Werther*, a last-minute substitution of tenors spoiled his evening. Bing left the box immediately before the announcement, unable to stand the pain of hearing the inevitable boos. Whenever guests arrived in his box, Bing would say, "You sit here and you sit there." Joan and I were smart enough to see from the outset that he was going to call the shots. When he had issued his orders, we didn't say, "Oh, wouldn't you see better if you sat here?" We didn't say a thing, we passed the test, and his permanently nervous state was not exacerbated.

I could gauge how vulnerable he was when on one occasion Maria Callas was with us in the box. She was obviously being difficult toward Bing. We all went up to the Grand Tier dining room during intermission, and he was trying to bury the hatchet after some squabble they had had. People in that dining room for a short interval usually ordered ice cream and cake: La Callas wanted a minute steak. When it finally came, her knife wasn't sharp enough. That struck me as a dangerous remark for her to make—dangerous for Bing (Scarpia had an easier time with Tosca). But we got through the crisis. Later in the evening, a crowd of well-wishers beneath the box began to applaud Callas. She asked me, "Vot shall I do?" I said, "Why don't you get up and bow to them?" She did, and I knew perfectly well that she had known what to do. She was just drawing out the pleasure of celebrity. For me it added a nuance to the term *prima donna*.

I didn't know quite how to thank Bing for being so kind to us with his invitations. Then I had an idea and did something unprecedented. I gave a party in the Scribner Book Store for Bing's book when it came out. That was the first time such a thing was done for someone not a Scribners author—for that matter, perhaps the first time one publisher launched another publisher's book. Our bookstore was a lovely place in which to give a cocktail party. The Doubleday people were flabbergasted, almost embarrassed. But I was pleased, and I hope Bing felt we had made some return for his many courtesies.

Malcolm Forbes was a neighbor of mine in Far Hills, New Jersey, and we used to play chess together. I would see him again at the Racquet Club, where we and a couple of other men would have lunch and then go to a Wednesday matinee. Malcolm and I became good friends, although I have the feeling that everything I ever did instinctively in relation to him was wrong. I thought some of his business ideas were wild, but he made more money than anybody since John D. Rockefeller. He was a type of genius I failed to recognize. His remarkable strengths I did not perceive. To think that I once gave him my views on the stock market makes me blush to remember it.

Malcolm Forbes wrote a book in 1978 called *The Sayings of Chairman Malcolm*, a collection of colorful wisdom bound in "banknote green" covers. No doubt it still outsells its Oriental "red" prototype.

After World War II he produced a book called *Nation's Heritage*, which was in fact a huge hardcover magazine for coffee tables and doctors' and lawyers' waiting rooms. It sold for one hundred dollars a volume. Much of the editorial material he gathered from publishers by getting the right to use illustrations. Nobody else would have thought of something so outrageous, but it succeeded without protest. It reminded me that when he was at Princeton, he started a slick magazine called the *Nassau Sovereign,* which also had quite a run.

It is clear that our friendship, Malcolm's and mine, must have been strong to survive our many differences. I don't like crowds, I don't like celebrity, I don't like the big time and the social scene. Nor am I what anybody would call savvy about business and moneymaking, in all of which he was a natural genius. For years, despite my fondness for him—or rather, because of it—I thought what he was doing, such as buying works of art as investments, was foolish. I thought his motorcycles and his balloons were expensive playthings. But his motorcycle agencies made a fortune. There's nothing that man touched that did not turn into gold.

Malcolm was a Scot, and spoke with a wry deliberateness. He had a great sense of the absurd and was excellent company.

I understand that at one time he was bound and determined to be President of the United States. When he was wounded as an infantryman in World War II, it was one of the great satisfactions of his life, because he knew it would be a great asset in his political career to have the Purple Heart. He also wanted to be governor of New Jersey. His friends and I used to kid him about it, calling him governor even after he lost the race in 1959. It was broad-minded of him not to resent having it rubbed in. Very possibly, if he had won then, he would have got the Presidency.

He had been one of those who helped persuade Eisenhower to run for the Presidency. Malcolm never had any fear of approaching anybody; he knew how to meet people and get things out of them in a way they did not resent. He knew how to get publicity; he was a meteor, a shooting star.

I am sorry that I never had the opportunity of meeting Scott Fitzgerald, who was one of the outstanding writers in the stable that Max Perkins had attracted to Scribners. Sometimes I feel that this extraordinary writer has been patronized by critics because of the excesses of the Jazz Age. Hemingway often criticized Fitzgerald for "prostituting" his talent by writing potboilers for magazines, but I can't help feeling that there was an element of *Schadenfreude* in Hemingway's endless allusions to Fitzgerald's drinking. The more I learn about Fitzgerald the more I admire him as a man and as an artist. In all the difficulties that came his way, he never shirked his responsibility to his daughter or his wife and was tireless in his efforts to support them by his writing. These moral strengths of the man were explained with wonderful clarity in the biography by Andrew Turnbull. How sad it is that Scott never lived to see the extraordinary success of his writings that developed during the 1950s. For many years, *The Great Gatsby* has been the best-selling novel in schools and colleges, having replaced *Silas Marner* as the quintessential novel for students (although Fitzgerald would not have appreciated the comparison). Year after year it has had the biggest sales of any Scribners book; in fact, it is the best-selling book in the history of our company.

In the seventies and early eighties my wife, Joan, and I used to make a regular scouting expedition to London twice a year in the hope of acquiring some exciting English books for Scribners. Jack Galazka, who was in charge of the trade department, usually got there a week ahead of us and by the time we arrived at the hotel, at night, there would be waiting for us several yellow-pad pages with Jack's words

"WELCOME TO LONDON!" at the top followed by a backbreaking schedule of meetings with authors, agents, and publishers, along with suggested dates for entertaining authors at lunch, tea, cocktails, and dinner. In addition there was a collection of manuscripts and books selected by Jack that needed to be read and considered without delay.

To help along with this, Joan volunteered to pitch in on the reading. She would spend several hours at this and then at breakfast would proudly hand over her assignment to Jack. He would thank her and smile encouragingly and then hand her another large batch from under his chair. It was impossible to keep ahead of him but Joan never stopped trying. He was great company throughout our visits.

In spite of all these strenuous days, we enjoyed ourselves immensely and I am happy to say that we never came back empty-handed; indeed, some of our very best books were the result of these transatlantic visits.

Acquisitions
and Mergers

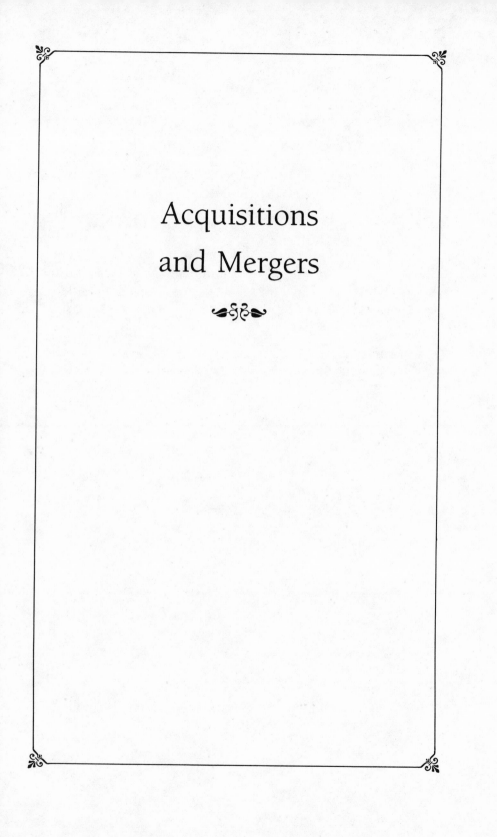

When I was a boy, it was always a treat for me to visit the Scribner Book Store. I remember the children's-book department, down in the back, with its tempting array. I have photographs of its "grandfather" store, on Broadway in the 1880s, with the books stacked in troughs that went for miles horizontally, to be picked up and examined by the customers. To me those photos convey the antiquity of the company even more than what I know of the publishing of those days.

Like the publishing company, the store went through the vicissitudes of the changing architecture and business life of New York City. My great-uncle, Ernest Flagg, who had designed the building at 155 Fifth Avenue that housed the store and the company, was the architect again when Scribners moved both operations up to 597 Fifth Avenue, near forty-eighth Street. He loved circular staircases, so the store had galleries above and two circular staircases to reach them. Fine editions and reference books were on a beautiful landing at the top of the stairs, and the children's books were down below.

After my father died, well-wishers pointed out to me that the bookstore needed a little primping up. It had what I might call theater windows, closed at the back so that the passerby couldn't see into the interior. We opened those up, and that in turn incited us to redecorate. We had the moldings on the ceiling gilded and bought bright-blue-and-white awnings for the front. The decorative ironwork on the façade was also regilded. It gave me the same pleasure as if I owned a gorgeous yacht.

We resisted all structural changes. Some interior-decorating wizards came to inspect and advise. They proposed that we put cove lighting around the arches so that they could be seen at night. In looking at my great-uncle's plans, they found that all the fixtures for cove lighting were already in place. But the bulbs had burned out, and either because of the cost during the Depression or because climbing that high is awkward work, the lights had never been replaced.

We did have to put in additional fixtures high up to increase the lighting, and we hired a firm to drill the holes. What *they* found was that my great-uncle had followed the manufacturing methods of the ancient Romans and put pebbles into the mix of the concrete. Drilling those holes, or rather, trying to drill, broke their bits. They couldn't get through. Rome wasn't built in a day, but it hasn't fallen apart in a day either. I enjoyed seeing how even older American standards could defeat modern efforts.

For some reason, we have had in the bookstore what might be called a White Russian tradition. First a man named Aldonov was made head of the store, and he brought in Igor Kropotkin, who had been born a prince in czarist Russia. When Soviet citizens visited the store, Igor would serve as interpreter. For the fun of it, in Stalin's day, Igor would ask visiting Russians if we should stock *Pravda*.

Another Russian, Nicholas Werden, headed the bookstore at one point and went on to become president of the American Booksellers Association. Werden, who had brought some

Russian writers into the Scribners orbit, got into a row with my father and left on short notice not long before I took charge. The abrupt break was a little embarrassing to me, because Werden and I were both members of the Book Table luncheon club, where we were bound to meet. But he took it in stride and so did I.

The Russian connection had another aspect, unrelated to the store and its management. My father, though an Episcopalian, was a trustee of the Russian Orthodox Church in New York City. This came about because of his White Russian friends, who asked him to help prevent Stalin from taking over the church.

For many New Yorkers in those more leisurely days, the Scribner Book Store was not just a shop but an institution. Sometimes when I was standing outside, I would hear people say, "That's the Scribner Book Store," as if pointing out a noteworthy sight. New York City was tardy about recognizing it as a landmark, but as an institution it played a special role beyond that of distributing books. Many a young woman just out of college who wanted to get a foot in the world of business would apply for a selling job there. I think a Rockefeller descendant worked for us at one time, and even debutantes condescended to make their apprenticeship in that decor of gaily jacketed books and lavish spaciousness.

The man in charge of the rare-book department, David Randall, was the panjandrum of the place. He was a great raconteur and I enjoyed stopping by to talk with him. He told me, for example, that he had sold the text of Lee's parting words to his troops—that surrender was inevitable —to a man who wanted to put it up in his own home. For what reason? To express *his* surrender to superior (domestic) forces. On another occasion, a distinguished-looking lady came in and said she wanted "a book of memorabilia." A very learned employee was grateful for the unusual phrasing of the wish, and asked if she would prefer Pepys's *Diary*, or Evelyn's. No, neither one: her daughter was getting married, and she needed a book to preserve the clippings. Our man lost his composure and exclaimed, "Jesus Christ! She wants a scrapbook!" He walked away unable to control his feelings.

Randall occupied a space at the back that could only be reached by going downstairs. There he met the book lovers and book collectors. He usually used the soft sell. If, for example, he knew that someone collected books about Chatterton, Randall would first talk to him about a lot of other things. Then *en passant* he would say, "Now here is a book just come to light, but it probably won't interest you." Once that man had the thing in his hands, it was certain he would not let it go and would buy it.

The most important rare book we ever had was a Gutenberg Bible. It occasioned one of my keenest disappointments. I wanted to put it in the window with a label saying it was the first book ever printed, but a pundit on the staff pulled scholarship on me and declared it wasn't the first. I dearly wanted to bend scholarship, just a little. A passerby would have so much pleasure looking in at our window and seeing the book that *ought to have been* the first ever printed.

We sold the Bible to Arthur Houghton, and in the sale we got back a fragmentary Bible, of which parts had apparently been used in Germany to wrap cuts of meat. Some of the books were complete, notably Job. About that same time, Randall was commissioned to sell for the General Theological Seminary its Gutenberg Bible. It went to Estelle Doheny, who was a Roman Catholic and who wanted it for the celebration of the Marian Year. But the Protestant seminary then decided not to let the sale go through, although one of its own trustees had engineered it. For a while we had the

Bible and no customer; now we had a customer and no Bible.

There was a further twist. The seminary's Bible turned out to be imperfect: the page dealing with the Whore of Babylon was a forgery, presumably made because the original page had been destroyed. Suddenly, Randall (and Scribners) were sitting pretty, because we had the missing page. Randall said it was a new element of uniqueness—we could set any price we wanted; there had never been a Gutenberg perfected in such a way. My sister's husband was on the faculty of the seminary and I reported the facts to him, but I added my assurance that we would not take advantage: "We'll give you the page. It's not worth anything to us other than one more page of a broken-up Bible, but to you it is the perfecting item and therefore priceless." Randall was annoyed at losing our chance to make a killing.

Shortly after that, he went to Indiana University, where he helped to build up their great Lilly Library. His replacement at Scribners, a man named Graves, served only for a short time because lack of capital and increasing rare-book prices compelled us to close the rare-book section.

Much later, during the 1970s, we expanded our services by putting in a paperback section. We lodged it in the building we owned behind the store, breaking through the wall to make the space one vast area. Where the rare books had been, we put a children's-book department with miniature desks and tables to make it attractive for the young readers. On the walls we had murals painted and we hung some of N. C. Wyeth's illustrations from *The Mysterious Island* and other books. The effort proved to be a noble failure because at that time, the heyday of Golden Books, people bought only low-priced editions for their children. Traffic through our little Parnassus was pitifully small.

Our next thought was to open branches around the country. The bookstore was a division of the company, but we spun it off as a separate entity so as to enable us to franchise it. In the early 1970s, a Scribner bookstore opened in Williamsburg, Virginia, which is still there (renamed Rizzoli), and one in Denver, Colorado, which is no longer in operation. By and large the undertaking did not answer our expectations, but I should add that there is now a Scribner Book Store in Costa Mesa, California, and another in Washington, D.C.—with more branches soon to sprout, under its new B. Dalton ownership.

The difficulty independent bookstores face today is that they can no longer afford to pay the rent it takes to have enough space for sufficient stock. The unit of sale is too small. In a clothing store, a customer pays several hundred dollars in one purchase; in a bookstore most items can be bought for under twenty. It was by this arithmetic that Scribners was finally forced into a series of decisions about the store, and indeed about the company, that were wrenching to make.

The first was to sell the bookstore to Rizzoli in 1984. There was really no alternative. On Fifth Avenue, it is virtually impossible, as later events have shown, to maintain a lavish bookstore in the teeth of sky-high real estate values. At the time we sold both the building and the store, the store alone was costing the family something like $500,000 a year to subsidize. To keep it going would have meant becoming patrons to the carriage trade.

In the Scribners administrative structure, I was for many years president of the company and chief executive officer. My cousin George Schieffelin was treasurer. He had worked at the Scribner Press for a while, and after my father died, became treasurer as his father had been before him.

As colleagues in the business, we worked as equal partners, though I had a preponderance of the stock. George was very supportive. He complained only occasionally about some of my mistakes or rash impulses. When he learned that I had sold our shares in Grosset & Dunlap at cost, he never remonstrated over the passed-up profit. "Most of it would have gone to taxes anyway" was his exaggerated consolation. With the people in the company, he was very popular, though not at all a literary type of man. When he died in 1988, many former employees of Scribners came to his funeral to show their respect and affection for him.

Lee Rodgers, a graduate of the University of Pennsylvania, who had come into the firm to work with George, helped us in so many ways that I eventually suggested to him that he become president and chief operating officer of the company. I would become chairman of the board and remain its chief executive officer. He served us faithfully in all business matters and with such evident success that he was eventually snapped up by Warner Communications.

Most publishers used to print their own books. Scribners did until the 1950s in the plant on West Forty-third Street. But the economic odds turned against any such operation when more and more expensive capital equipment came to be needed for efficiency. Our manufacturing building, too, was poorly laid out. Books had to be lugged from one floor to another, which is called jackassing, instead of being movable horizontally through the various steps in production. Moreover, there was not enough room for stock.

We closed the plant down, but saw to it that no one was laid off who didn't have another job. Then we built a large warehouse in Totowa, New Jersey, from which we did our shipping and billing. This attractive new facility was somewhat bigger than we needed, so we decided to dilute the overhead by taking on shipping for other publishers. We signed up Serge Obolensky, Harry Abrams, and Alfred (Pat) Knopf, Jr., who had started a new company called Atheneum.

Pat Knopf and I must have met sometime after World War II. He had distinguished himself as a bomber pilot flying out of England. Pat is a very gregarious person, and we had meals together from time to time. I always thought of him warmly as a friendly acquaintance. Our situations were much alike as heirs each to a notable family business. Alfred Knopf and his Borzoi Books were internationally famous. I knew Alfred Senior very well, and had great respect for him. He had not only been kind to me and sympathetic to what we did in publishing, but he shared to the full my love of books as books.

When Alfred Knopf was a student at Columbia, he used to come into the Scribner Book Store and hobnobbed there with an old Scribners person named Simpson, who was already old when Alfred was a boy. I heard about this bookish connection from Alfred himself much later. I said, "Alfred, he's down there in the store now. He's probably in his shivering nineties." And indeed he was. Alfred went down and talked to him, and the man said, "Oh, yes, I remember you when you were a student at Columbia." Scribners keeps its people from almost the cradle to the edge of the grave.

Mr. Knopf, who was considered the greatest gourmet in New York, sometimes asked me to lunch at his place. Often what was served seemed to me rather meager, such as a delicate sandwich and some fruit. Much as I loved Alfred and respected his authority about food, on those occasions I felt the lack of something a little more filling. I would have settled for a hot dog. At other times, he took me to the St. Regis, where I had freer scope. Our conversations tended to dwell on the current trends in publishing. He regretted the passing of the ways of my grandfather's and father's generations. He was particularly unhappy about the vogue of the pornographic element in fiction. "Some of these books," he would say, "you have to pick up with a pair of tongs." He was also annoyed at the role of agents, who now dominated the scene.

Alfred was by nature an autocrat. When he merged his firm with Bennett Cerf's at Random House, they got along extremely well, but it was yet another change in his professional life that he found hard to swallow. He was moreover unhappy about the difference of opinion with his son, which had led the younger Knopf to form his own publishing company, Atheneum.

We at Scribners always got along well with Pat Knopf, and it occurred to us that we might increase our business by adding to ours that of another established company. We proposed a friendly takeover to Pat, and Atheneum became part of what we called the Scribner Book Companies. He took the title of vice-chairman. Marvin Brown, who was Pat Knopf's treasurer, became treasurer of the consortium.

The Atheneum imprint of course continued. The firm had been organized by Pat, Simon Bessie, and Hiram Haydn, the editor of *The American Scholar*. I knew all three. Owing to its small size, Atheneum had had some difficulty surviving in the heavy-hitting publishing scrimmage. They had some splendid books coming through Bessie, Haydn, and Knopf, among them a few big sellers at the start. But the going got rough when interest rates went up and up. Those were difficult times for anybody in any business, only more so for publishers, because it is an inventory business—most of the money is tied up in masses of books on warehouse shelves. Hence bank loans are unavoidable and rates as high as twenty percent in the late 1970s proved devastating to many publishers.

In these circumstances, Atheneum's contribution to sales and editorial strength was valuable support. The arrangement was equally welcome to Pat. He was virtually autonomous, and he took full advantage of his situation. By nature ferociously independent, he resisted the established procedures of the new company. It was not that he didn't bring in many good books; it was just that the company was not well integrated. Pat was clearly not comfortable unless he was totally in charge.

By the time of the merger, Haydn and Bessie had fallen off along the way. Haydn was not strong on procuring books. He was a very literate man, who wrote several books himself and taught a course in publishing. I think it was part of his character to want to be mentor and revered uncle to young people. He consequently overvalued the work of the young he came across. Maxwell Perkins had the same desire to help along, but Perkins applied a stronger mind to judging books.

Atheneum brought Rawson Associates with it into the Scribner Book Companies. Ken Rawson was a knowledgeable publisher, and his wife, Eleanor, was among the best editors of "practical" books. The Rawsons have a preternatural gift for unearthing and promoting great best-sellers. They published *The Status Seekers* and *Everything You Always Wanted to Know About Sex but Were Afraid to Ask*. Their diet books swept the country, including *The Complete Scarsdale Diet* and *Eat to Win*. When they came into our joint companies with a string of publishing triumphs to their name, they probably had as many books on the best-seller list as anyone in the trade.

The idea behind the formation of the Scribner Book Companies was that it would be a mother ship. In the carrying out of the plan, it divided our resources. We had wanted to enlarge our scope because we had a huge shipping and fulfillment plant, which had become something of a white elephant. We took on other partners there to spread the costs, but it never occurred to me to have our shipping done by another firm. I considered the warehouse a fixture that couldn't be moved, just as my predecessors had seen printing at the Scribner Press. If I were advising a young publisher today, I would tell him that what seems unthinkable should be thought about. Had I not been so concerned with volume of business, and had I farmed out our shipping as we did our printing, Scribners might still exist today as an independent company.

Since we were doing the distribution of Atheneum books before the merger, we should have had a head start in combining the sales forces; Pat had brought Nat Zecker into Scribners as sales manager, but the fact that he came in specifically for Atheneum sales within the company indicated that what we had was a confederation rather than an honest-to-God merger.

Pat had brought on board a number of major authors, such as James Clavell and Dan Jenkins, but unfortunately Atheneum wasn't able to keep the stronger ones. Nobody could fault Pat for it. It was a period when agents and other publishers made keeping authors a life-and-death struggle. Writers became nomads, continually lured to a greener oasis by the mirage of huge royalties prophesied by agents or offered by editors.

In any case, mergers are always difficult. If all the parties are on the *qui vive* for their rights, it gets to be like the confederation of American states before the Constitutional Convention. In a personal, variable, and inexact business like publishing, where intuition rather than provable argument plays a major role, the opportunities for disunion are ever-present. In short, the Scribner Book Companies merger was not running smoothly. The financial pressure was great; we felt menaced by bank loans and debt; and I had an anguished concern for our employees, though I had set up a good retirement plan.

I also lost two valuable lieutenants: Lee Rodgers, who had been president of Scribners, and Marvin Brown, who had been Atheneum's president. Marvin became president of the New American Library, and Lee Rodgers president of Warner Publishing Services. We parted amicably, but then I found myself shorthanded, with no close advisers and helpers on the business side, except Jack Galazka and my son Charlie. He and I talked from time to time about the future of the family business and finally one day I made the decision that I wanted to merge with a bigger, stronger firm. I knew exactly which firm: I wanted to merge with Macmillan.

In our earliest days, Scribners had been the American representative for Macmillan, an English company. When I became head of Scribners, Macmillan had recently split and there was a new, independent, American Macmillan run by George Brett. He was a strict and strong-minded head of house. His oldest son, Platt Brett, I had known at St. Paul's School, and Bruce, the next in line, at a later time. I had dealings with the father at the American Book Publishers Council.

George Brett held crotchety views on copyright matters, acted dynastic, and was generally uncooperative, but in 1960 Macmillan went through a great upheaval that brought Raymond C. Hagel to the top. Macmillan was acquired by Collier's and I knew little of what followed, except that under Hagel the company expanded steadily into a large conglomerate. It did not do well and Thomas Mellon Evans, with his son Edward, bought the company in 1980. Ned Evans, who is my junior, became chairman of the board and stayed to run the company after his father sold his share.

During that era, the only contact I had with the firm was with Jeremiah Kaplan, the founder of the Free Press, who had become head of Macmillan Publishing. He and I had in common our strong interest in reference books. I had read and liked a number of Jerry's Free Press books, and when one day out of the blue he asked me to have lunch with him at Macmillan, I accepted. He had no apparent axe to grind. He is an intellectual, and I'm an intellectual, and we had a good time talking about publishing.

By the time I began to discuss with my son the possibility of a merger, we had already dispensed with the warehouse and had enlisted Macmillan to do our shipping and billing. With that link in mind and the memory of a nice lunch, I called Jerry and said I'd like to see him. In his office, after taking off my hat and sitting down, I said, "I wonder if you would be interested in taking over Scribners?" He said, "That's the most exciting thing I've ever heard in my life." I told him that our lists and our enthusiasms matched perfectly. The close fit would make a merger extraordinarily opportune.

Jerry did the negotiating for Macmillan, and Allan Rabinowitz, whom I had taken on as treasurer and later appointed president, represented Scribners. I had no interest in selling the company for cash, because I wanted to keep the firm in the book business and I wanted to maintain my commitment—financially as well as professionally—to a *publishing* company. The whole transaction was done in stock, which was probably one of the most advantageous ones I have made. The stock split and appreciated steadily, so that in four years it had reached six times the price at which it was quoted in 1984, the year of the merger.

A great load of responsibility was lifted from my shoulders by the move: my immediate family, George Schieffelin and his family, indeed all the members of the Scribner family, including my nieces and nephews who owned stock in the Scribner Book Companies, had been getting little out of it because we could not pay significant dividends. By my decision to merge with Macmillan I justified their patience. When Macmillan was finally bought by Robert Maxwell in late 1988, the value of Scribners stock was worth thirty-six times what it had been when I took over the management in 1952. As I have never thought of myself as a financier, it must have been my guardian angel who inspired the arrangement.

I think it has been an excellent acquisition for Macmillan, too. My dealings with Ned Evans and Bill Reilly, Macmillan's president, on the personnel policy of the company could not have been more agreeable and cooperative, and I noted with pleasure that they were soon friendly with Charlie, who later served them in various capacities.

Macmillan took on the Scribners sales force for trade books—extremely good people—as well as most of the salesmen in the reference department. The same arrangements were made for as many clerical workers as possible, and most of our editors were also retained.

After the merger, I stayed on as chairman of the Scribners board, and kept a *de facto* role as the director of Scribners' reference books. The Scribners imprint is retained. Jerry Kaplan brought in someone to run Scribners' trade publishing, while the reference-book and children's-book departments came under the Macmillan wing.

I still maintain a strong interest in Scribner Reference Books and attend the sales conferences as often as possible as a cheerleader. I am especially happy that the present publisher of Scribner Reference Books is Karen Day, who joined the company in 1977 after graduating from Smith College. But feeling that I was not doing my share in the day-to-day work of the company, I have taken myself off the payroll. I work as a volunteer, for the sheer pleasure of staying in publishing: I like the business which is also a profession. This fact has probably been apparent. At the same time, I enjoy the unaccustomed relief from pressure.

My son is the fifth Charles Scribner, and, although he was in the line of succession as head of the firm, he favored the merger without reservations. I think he had long been concerned about the electrical crosscurrents and lack of spiritual coordination that prevailed within Scribners after the merger with Atheneum. And he was completely objective about the difficulties the company would continue to face now that its private ownership had been extended beyond the Scribner family. He clearly preferred a benevolent corporate parent to a divided board of directors and an undercapitalized future.

Macmillan took Charlie on as assistant to the president and he apprenticed under Jerry Kaplan. Besides being a good writer, with two books and several published papers in art history to his credit, Charlie is a natural diplomat and troubleshooter. I think of him as a utility outfielder for the Macmillan management. After the merger he took over personal responsibility for our key backlist authors and their estates, above all Hemingway and Fitzgerald, and has remained an active member of Scribners' editorial department.

My two younger sons, Blair and John, chose more independent careers to pursue. I cannot help reflecting that in so doing they fulfilled avocations of both their father and grandfather. Blair became a teacher, which had been my own first choice of profession back in my Princeton days. John is an artist, a career my father might have chosen had not his parents removed those pencils and paints at the earliest sign of interest. As for my two spirited grandsons, Charlie (sixth in the line) and Christopher, I dare not venture a guess: we have yet to produce a rock singer, or a professional wrestler. But their mother, Ritchie, is a talented painter as well as a former teacher, which may well reinforce those family traditions for another generation.

*   *   *

When I recount all the things that I pruned from Scribners, including the printing plant, warehouse, bookstore, and building, I feel somewhat like Attila the Hun, because at first sight it looks as if I had lopped off, rather than built and enlarged. But as Seneca said, "Fate leads the willing and drags the unwilling." Modern economic conditions spin the fate that controls the life of business firms—especially family-owned companies. The time had come when Scribners would either be led or dragged; I preferred to be led. I feel no sense of disappointment. Scribners is still a respected imprint under which many splendid and entertaining books appear and succeed in both the commercial and the cultural domains. My forebears, I am confident, would be delighted by so happy an outcome—and so promising a prospect.

Several years ago my wife, Joan, and I built a cottage in rural Bedminster, New Jersey. We planned to use it on weekends and vacations. The house was erected in the middle of an open field and there was no landscaping—only the wild trees, shrubs, and weeds that happened to be growing there. These were the creation of Mother Nature in one of her least inspired moods. But that did not bother me. The whole place was delightfully informal compared with the city.

I told Joan that we did not need a lawn. It would be a mistake to plan one. I had always thought that the Japanese had the right approach to such things and I was taken with the idea of a garden consisting of a patch of bare sand planted with a few rocks. Joan made no comment, which is a tactically sound, if slightly unfair, position to take toward a husband's ideas.

Well, it soon became crystal clear that we could not possibly get by with *no* lawn. The ground in front of the house was a sea of mud left by the builders and we would need to put down sod as quickly as possible unless we were willing to wear wooden shoes most of the time.

We began with a very small lawn for that limited purpose, and I bought a very small hand lawnmower, since even the smallest lawn has to be mowed from time to time. For a while all was clear sailing, but one fateful day it occurred to me that the fields that surrounded our little lawn looked messy. The grass and weeds stood about three feet high. Just as an "experiment" I would crop them down. Nothing like a lawn, of course; I'd just make them a little less wild.

This experiment worked very well, and as the result of it I made a profound horticultural discovery: every hayfield is a potential lawn. Philosophically speaking, a hayfield is a lawn *in posse*. You do not need seed, or fertilizer, or anything. All you need to do is keep it mowed. It looked so beautiful to me cut short that way that I could not bear the thought of ever letting it grow back.

At this point it was clear that since I had enlarged the lawn considerably, I would need more than a small hand mower. So I bought a gasoline-powered mower—the kind you have to push. That made cutting the grass so easy that I found myself enlarging the lawn further by nibbling away at the new boundary between lawn and fields, and thus creating a larger and larger area of what the French call a *tapis vert*.

In mathematics, this nibbling is referred to as an "iterative process": you keep on doing the same thing and eventually you really get somewhere. I soon reached the point where the lawn could be measured in acres rather than square feet and the power mower that I was pushing around needed to be replaced by a tractor mower—the kind you sit on. With that marvelous machine huge areas of field could be transformed into lawn with even less effort than before. Our property was beginning to look like a park and I loved it more and more. But I found that I was now spending at least half of every weekend riding around on a Cub Cadet. Life in the country had become an ordeal of taming Mother Nature and keeping her that way. The time it was taking would soon have to be limited or I'd be obliged to give up my job in New York. It was time to call a halt. So I finally enclosed the whole lawn with a post-and-rail fence: it was one way to set a limit to further expansion. I also made a vow to myself that from then on *nothing* on the other side of that fence would be beautified by me in any way, no matter how wild and woolly it might look.

I can summarize this experience in landscaping by a modest revision of Occam's razor: *A lawn must not be extended beyond one's ability to keep it cut.*

It seems to me that the entire domain of the intellect—that is, the sum total of all our knowledge and skills, our languages, and our arts and sciences—can be compared to a great lawn. Both lawn and scholarship are man-made; and because of the peculiarities of human nature, both have strong tendencies to expand. But while the expansion of a lawn can be stopped by something as simple as the decision to put up a fence, the thrust of the creative imagination cannot be controlled by anything comparable. There seems to be no way to prevent the human mind from pushing forward the edges of knowledge and experience. Every area of the unknown, the untamed, or the incomprehensible presents a challenge. And there will always be a number of gifted individuals—artists or scientists, scholars or philosophers—who will wish to move into that wild outer area to rationalize and humanize it.

As in an expanding lawn, the expanding of the domain of the intellect makes possible a distinction between the relatively old areas and the new ones. The older areas contain the heritage of the past, the major artistic and intellectual achievements of earlier generations. Those areas of learning cannot be neglected without unfortunate consequences to society. Like a neglected lawn they will rapidly go to seed. A serious symptom of present-day neglect in this area is the deterioration of the language. It is a sign that one of the fundamental arts and needs of civilization itself is at risk. This in turn is a warning that the other basics must be rescued as well. Thus there is an ever-present need for better teachers and better students, better libraries and better laboratories. Our mowing must keep pace with our growing.

The frontier territory is the place where our best artists, scholars, and writers spend the most important parts of their lives—so that they may enrich and broaden ours. It is why a lifetime in their company has never seemed too long.

Index

❦